Everything Patchwork

Everything Patchwork

40 classic quilts, bags and accessories

Corinne Crasbercu

Photography by Hiroko Mori
Styling by Vania Leroy-Thuillier

MURDOCH BOOKS

Contents

Basic sewing box — what you'll need

Always have your sewing box close at hand when you start work; it will make whatever you are doing easier. Also make sure it is always complete. There is nothing is more annoying than having to stop sewing to go hunting for the right pair of scissors or worse, having to run to the sewing-supplies store to buy missing embroidery cotton.

- needles for hand sewing
- needles for machine sewing
- blunt-end and sharp embroidery needles
- safety pins (for quilting)
- pins
- an assortment of threads in different colours for hand sewing
- an assortment of threads in different colours for machine sewing
- an assortment of stranded embroidery cottons
- special machine quilting thread in black and white
- tailor's chalk or erasable pencil for fabric
- a pair of sewing scissors
- a pair of embroidery scissors
- tape measure and ruler
- embroidery hoop
- knitting needle (for turning ties and handles inside-out more easily)
- iron and ironing board
- spray bottle (for steam-ironing)
- sewing machine

A few metres of fabric, plain or with floral patterns, soft and pretty, small off-cuts of vintage prints picked up from second-hand stores or car boot sales, buttons, ribbons and transfers, a basic sewing box, and you can start.

I have made all these pieces using only traditional patchwork patterns, but I have adapted them. There are no complicated shapes, no overly technical construction nor overly restrictive stitches, just the pleasure of playing with fabrics, combining them with novel accessories and customising them.

The one and only motto for the pieces in this book is: have fun and take pleasure in making these projects for yourself, your friends or your home.

Quilts, bags and other accessories

Mushroom pincushions

instructions
p. 66

Cupcake pincushion p. 67

Sewing kit
instructions
p. 68

Strawberry pincushion

instructions
p. 72

Bunting

instructions
p. 78

Zippered purse and make-up bag

instructions p. 80-81

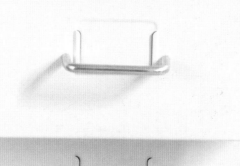

instructions
p. 84

Hexagon quilted cover

instructions p. 85

Flowers cushion Instructions p. 88

Dreams cushion

instructions
p. 89

Rose tote bag

instructions
p. 94

Bordered basket and rosette

instructions
p. 95 & 100

Home sweet home decoration instructions p. 101

Small quilted bag

p. 103

Diary cover

p. 105

Tissue case

p. 108

Mobile phone pouch

instructions
p. 109

Placemat

instructions p. 110

Flower tea cosy

instructions
p. 112

41

Bird tea cosy

instructions p. 113

42

Kitchen pocket wall-hanging

instructions p. 118

Recipe book cover

Instructions p. 120

Little sugar pots

Instructions p. 121

Striped apron

instructions
p. 122

Shoulder bag

p. 128

Assorted cushions

Instructions p. 130-132

Laundry bag

instructions p. 136

Heart sachet

Instructions
p. 137

instructions
p. 140

pegbag

100 %
COTTON

Instructions and patterns

Machine-sewn quilt [photo page 10]

1 basic sewing box (see page 6)
12 pieces of cotton fabric with different prints, to cut 60 x 12.5 cm squares
70 x 100 cm quilt wadding
62 x 92 cm pink-and-white polkadot cotton, for the backing
310 x 5 cm blue cotton with tiny hearts, for the binding

Cut 60 squares from the 12 different pieces of fabric: 40 squares along the straight grain and 20 squares on the bias for the edges. The quilt is constructed 'on point' as follows: Starting with two bias squares in one corner, lay out the squares in rows, adding two extra squares in each subsequent row until you reach the two middle rows, which have 10 squares each, then decreasing in the same way back to the diagonally oppposite corner (10 rows in total). The corner squares and the square on each end of each row should be a bias square.

Move the squares around until you are happy with the colour placement, but always keep the bias squares at the edges. Allowing 1-cm seams, join the squares together into rows, pressing the seam allowances for each row in alternate directions.

Now sew the rows together, matching the seams. Do not trim the edges yet.

Lay the backing fabric out flat, wrong side up, place the wadding on top, then centre the patchwork, right side up, on top and pin with safety pins. (The edges of the top will extend beyond the other layers.) Working by hand or machine, quilt around the inside of every second square (see techniques on page 142). When the quilting is complete, carefully trim the sides through all layers, to make a 62 x 92 cm rectangle. Each outer bias square will now become a triangle with the straight grain along the edge.

With right sides together, pin the binding around the edge of the quilt, making mitred corners, then stitch and press (see techniques on page 142).

Scissor holders [photo page 11]

Red Riding Hood

1 basic sewing box (see page 6)
28 x 20 cm blue cotton with small white hearts, for the outside
28 x 20 cm white cotton, for the lining
28 x 20 cm thin fusible quilt wadding
1 'Red Riding Hood' motif
45 cm red rickrack
40 cm x 5 mm-wide red gingham ribbon
1 small white heart-shaped 2-hole button

Fuse the wadding to the wrong side of the heart-print fabric (see techniques on page 142). Using the pattern on page 64, cut two Scissors Holders from each of the fused fabric and the lining fabric, remembering to add a 1-cm margin all around to allow for the seams.

Sew the motif onto one of the pieces for the outside of the holder, using large running stitches and red stranded cotton. Place the outer pieces together, right sides facing each other, and stitch 1 cm from the edge, leaving the top curved edges open. Do the same for the lining, but leave an opening in one straight side.

Slip the lining inside the outer case, right sides together, and stitch around the opening edges, allowing a 1-cm seam. Turn the holder right side out through the opening in the lining and press, then sew the opening closed by hand and push the lining back inside the holder.

Pin and then sew a small rickrack border around the opening edges, on the inside. Cut the ribbon in two and sew one end of each piece to the front and back of the holder, in the middle, so the holder can be tied closed. Sew a small heart-shaped button above the motif using red stranded cotton.

Cat

1 basic sewing box (see page 6)
28 x 20 cm novelty print blue cotton, for the outside
28 x 20 cm white cotton, for the lining
28 x 20 cm thin fusible quilt wadding
1 'Cat' motif
45 cm x 15 mm-wide red gingham bias binding
40 cm x 5 mm-wide red satin ribbon
1 small white round 4-hole button

Fuse the wadding to the wrong side of the novelty print fabric (see techniques on page 142). Using the pattern on page 64, cut two Scissors Holders from each of the fused fabric and the lining fabric, remembering to add a 1-cm margin on the straight sides to allow for the seams, but not around the curved edges of the opening (as these will be bound).

Baste the motif onto one of the pieces for the outside of the holder, and quilt in place by outlining some of the features (see techniques page 142). Place the outer pieces together, right sides facing each other, and stitch 1 cm from the edge, leaving the top curved

edges open. Do the same for the lining. Press, then turn the outer holder right side out and slip the lining inside, wrong sides together and seams matching. Bind around the opening edges with gingham bias binding.

Cut the ribbon in two and sew one end of each piece to the front and back of the holder, in the middle, so the holder can be tied closed. Sew a small white round button above the motif using red thread.

Scissors holders

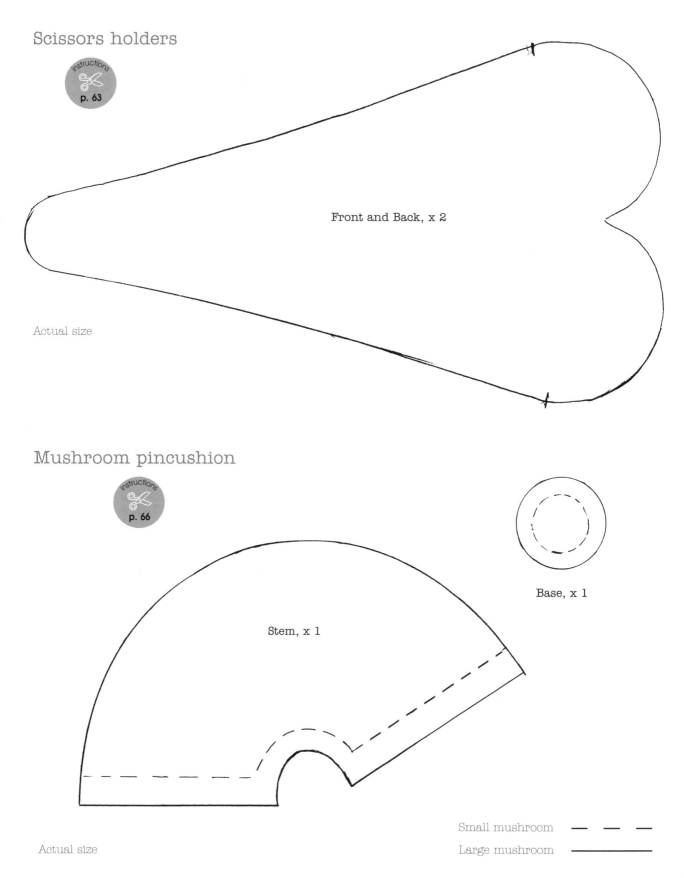

instructions ✂ p. 63

Front and Back, x 2

Actual size

Mushroom pincushion

instructions ✂ p. 66

Base, x 1

Stem, x 1

Actual size

Small mushroom — — — —

Large mushroom ————

64

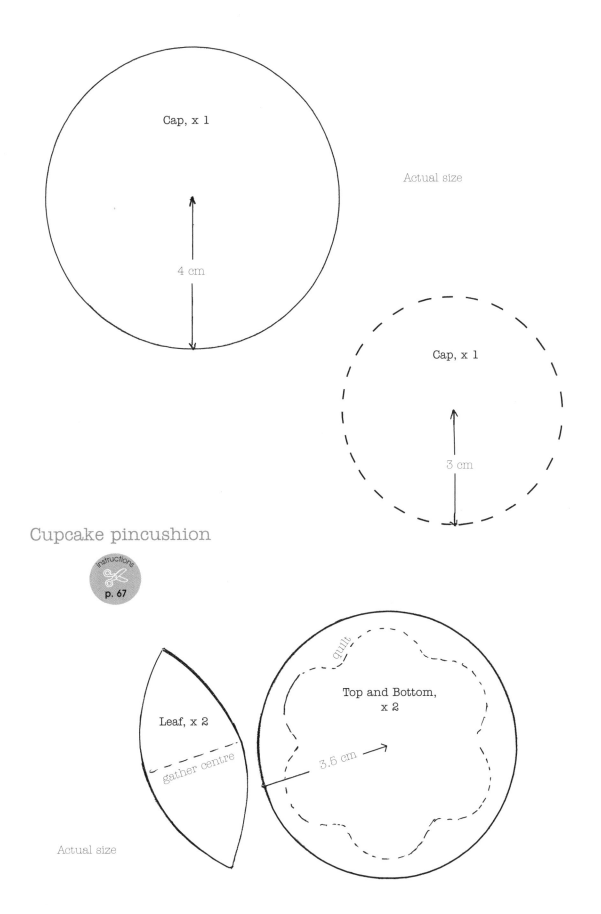

Cap, x 1

Actual size

4 cm

Cap, x 1

3 cm

Cupcake pincushion

Instructions

p. 67

quilt

Top and Bottom,
x 2

Leaf, x 2

gather centre

3.5 cm

Actual size

Mushroom pincushion [photo page 12]

Large mushroom

1 basic sewing box (see page 6)
15 x 15 cm white cotton, for the stem and base
a little synthetic filling
27 x 5 cm white cotton, for the underside of the cap
10 cm-diameter circle of red cotton with small white polkadots, for the top of the cap
10 cm dark-green rickrack

Small mushroom

1 basic sewing box (see page 6)
13 x 13 cm white cotton, for the stem and base
a little synthetic filling
21 x 4.5 cm white cotton, for the underside of the cap
8 cm-diameter circle of red cotton with large red polkadots, for the top of the cap
8 cm light-green rickrack

Using the patterns on page 64, cut out the stem of the mushroom from the square of white cotton and a circle for the base, remembering to add a 1-cm margin all round to allow for the seams. Join the two straight sides of the stem, stitching 1 cm from the edge. Pin the white cotton base circle to the narrow end of the stem, right sides together, and sew 1 cm from the edge. Turn right side out and, using double thread, sew a running stitch gathering line around the open edge, 1 cm from the edge. Stuff the stem with filling, turn in the edge 1cm and pull up the gathering thread tightly to gather the top of the stem.

Fold the white cotton rectangle for the underside of the cap in half, bringing the short sides together, and stitch 1 cm from the short edge. With right sides together, pin the edge of the polkadot circle to one end of this tube and stitch, 1 cm from the edge. Turn right side out. Sew a gathering thread all around the opening as before, 1 cm from the edge, stuff the cap with filling, fold the fabric in 1 cm and pull up the gathering thread to draw up the opening. The base of the cap and the top of the stem should be the same circumference.

Pin the cap and the stem together and sew them to each other by hand, using small fine stitches. Sew a rickrack trim around the bottom of the stem.

Cupcake pincushion [photo page 14]

1 basic sewing box (see page 6)
24 cm light-green rickrack
9 cm-diameter circle of red floral print cotton, for the bottom, and 1 rectangle,
   24 x 5 cm, for the sides
9 cm-diameter circle of red-and-white polkadot cotton, for the top
10 x 10 cm thin cotton wadding
a little synthetic filling
small piece light-green felt
1 small red ball-shaped button or bead

Sew the rickrack along the middle of the rectangle of floral fabric, on the right side, then fold the fabric in half, bringing the two short sides together, right sides facing each other. Make a tube by stitching the short sides together, 1 cm from the edge, leaving a 2-cm opening in the middle of the seam.

Place the circle of polkadot fabric on the wadding and quilt (see techniques on page 142) as indicated on the pattern (see page 65), then trim the wadding to the size of the circle.

With right sides together, pin the quilted circle of fabric to one end of the floral fabric tube and the floral circle to the other end, and stitch, 1 cm from the edges. Turn right side out through the side opening, stuff with synthetic filling, then sew the opening closed by hand.

Following the pattern on page 64, cut a leaf shape from light-green felt without adding seam allowance. Sew a line of running stitch across the middle of the leaf, as indicated, draw up the thread to gather it and tie off securely. Sew the leaf to the centre top of the cupcake. Sew a small ball-shaped button or bead on top of the leaf.

Sewing kit [photo page 15]

1 basic sewing box (see page 6)
31 x 29 cm floral cotton, for the large interior pocket
25 cm x 5 mm-wide flat elastic
2 rectangles light fusible wadding, each 27 x 32 cm
27 x 32 cm blue gingham, for the inside
27 x 32 cm red-and-white polkadot cotton, for the outside, 27 x 9.5 cm, for the small pocket,
   and 2 strips, each 22 x 5 cm, for the handles
6 x 7 cm novelty print cotton, for the small button pocket
25 cm x 5 mm-wide red-and-white spotted ribbon, for the cotton reels
2 fabric motifs
5 cm linen ribbon
2 very small white flat 4-hole buttons
4 novelty buttons
1 small novelty 'scissors' badge (optional)

Following the measurements on the diagram (opposite), cut the floral fabric to the shape of the large interior pocket. Remember to add a 1-cm margin on each side to allow for the seams and a 2-cm margin at the top and bottom for the hems.

Make a 1-cm double hem at the top and bottom of the floral fabric. Insert a piece of elastic through the hem at the bottom and pull up to reduce the width to 25 cm. Firmly stitch the the end of the elastic on each side.

Fuse a rectangle of light wadding to the wrong side of the gingham (see techniques on page 142). Lay the floral fabric pocket on the gingham, wrong side of pocket against right side of gingham, and stitch the pocket divisions as indicated on the diagram.

Make a 1-cm double hem along one long edge of the 27 x 9.5 cm rectangle of polkadot fabric, and on the top edge of the novelty print button pocket. Press under 1 cm on the remaining edges of this button pocket and topstitch it to the centre of the polkadot rectangle.

With right sides together, position the polkadot rectangle on the floral interior pocket, placing the raw edge of the rectangle 9.5 cm below the top of the floral fabric. Stitch along the polkadot fabric, 1 cm from the edge, then fold this rectangle back over the seam onto the floral fabric and stitch the vertical division of the pocket, as indicated.

Make a buttonhole (see techniques on page 142) at each end of the red-and-white spotted ribbon, using 2 strands of red stranded cotton, then attach this ribbon to the pocket, in the middle, so that you can thread cotton reels onto it from each side.

Make handles from the two strips of polkadot fabric (see techniques on page 142).

Fuse the second rectangle of light wadding to the wrong side of the large polkadot rectangle (see techniques on page 142). Place the gingham rectangle on top of the polkadot rectangle, right sides together and raw edges matching. Insert the handles at the top and bottom between the two layers, so that the two ends of each handle will be sewn into the seams. Fold the linen ribbon into a loop and insert the ends between the layers at the centre of the upper edge. Stitch all around, 1 cm from the edge, leaving an opening on one side.

Turn right side out, sew the opening closed by hand and press. To finish, sew a small white button onto the floral fabric at each end of the red ribbon, so that you can secure the cotton reels. Sew a button to the outside of the kit, to correspond with the ribbon loop. Sew on the remaining buttons as desired.

Placement diagram for the sewing kit (all measurements are finished size)

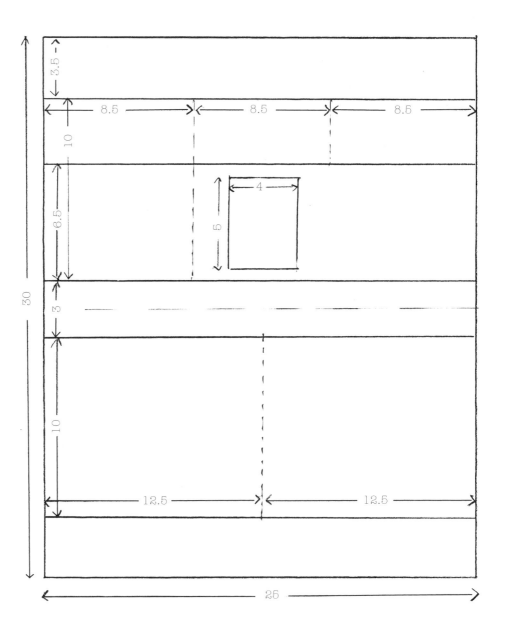

Placement diagram for the large interior pocket (all measurements are finished size)

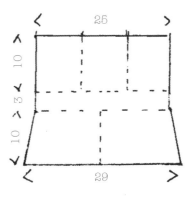

Pocket tidy [photos pages 16-17]

Wall tidy

1 basic sewing box (see page 6)
57 x 73 cm natural linen, for the front
57 x 73 cm red-and-white polkadot cotton, for the back, and 3 rectangles,
  each 50 x 18 cm, for the pocket linings
26 x 18 cm sky-blue-and-white polkadot cotton, for the lower pocket, 18 x 18 cm,
  for the middle pocket, and 3 x 18 cm, for the upper pocket
18 x 18 cm floral cotton for the middle pocket, and 28 x 18 cm, for the upper pocket
26 x 18 cm red-and-white striped fabric, for the lower pocket
18 x 18 cm large-checked red gingham, for the middle pocket
13 x 18 cm small-checked red gingham, for the upper pocket
4 vintage transfers
4 small pieces white cotton, slightly larger than the transfers
1.1 m x 90 cm-wide light fusible wadding
4.3 m red rickrack
52 cm x 40 mm-wide cotton 'tape measure' ribbon
53 cm x 35 mm-wide white twill tape or grosgrain ribbon
6 flat white 4-hole buttons
1 large fabric badge (see technique on page 143)
69 cm x 10 mm-diameter white dowel rod

Small bags

1 basic sewing box (see page 6)
12 x 24 cm red-and-white polkadot fabric
10.5 x 25 cm blue gingham
2 fabric motifs
50 cm x 5 mm-wide red gingham ribbon

Using the photograph as a guide and allowing 1-cm seams, sew the squares and rectangles of fabric together along their 18-cm edges to form the upper, middle and lower pockets. Cut and fuse (see techniques on page 142) a piece of wadding to the wrong side of each pocket.

Transfer the vintage images to the white cotton rectangles (see techniques on page 142), then press under all the raw edges and sew them by hand onto the pockets, using large running stitches and one strand of stranded cotton.

Place the rectangles of red polkadot lining fabric on top of the pockets, right sides together, and stitch all around, 1 cm from the edge, leaving an opening at the bottom. Turn right out, press, and sew a piece of rickrack along the top edge of each pocket.

Fuse some wadding to the wrong side of the large linen rectangle (see techniques on page 142). Turn under 1 cm on each end of the 'tape measure' ribbon, then centre the ribbon along the top of the linen rectangle, 6 cm from the upper edge, and topstitch in place.

Press under 1.5 cm on each end of the white tape or ribbon. Pin the ribbon along the top edge of the right side of the polkadot lining fabric, about 2.5 cm from the upper edge, to form a casing for the rod. Topstitch in place close to each long edge of the ribbon.

Place the front and back pieces of the pocket tidy together, right sides facing each other and raw edges matching, and stitch all around, 1 cm from the edge,

leaving an opening at the top. Turn right side out, sew the opening closed by hand and press.

Position the pockets on the front of the pocket tidy, placing the lower one 5 cm from the bottom and leaving a 4-cm space between each. Topstitch them to the backing fabric along the sides and bottom edge. Next, make vertical seams to create compartments.

Pin the rickrack around the edges and topstitch in place. Sew on a button at each corner, using red thread, and sew the remaining two buttons on the pockets, as shown.

Insert the rod into the casing and hang the pocket tidy on the wall using two hooks.

Sew the motifs to the two fabrics for the drawstring bags, so they are centred on the front of each bag. Fold the fabric rectangles for the bags in half, bringing the two short sides together, and stitch the sides, 1 cm from the edge, leaving a 1-cm opening 6 cm from the top in the seam on one side for the blue bag, and 2 cm from the top for the red bag. Press under 1 cm on the upper raw edge, then turn the pressed edge under again and pin so that the edge of the hem reaches the bottom of the side-opening. Stitch the hem in place close to the edge. For the blue bag, sew a second line of stitching, 1 cm above the first, to create a narrow casing.

Turn the bags right side out, thread a piece of ribbon through each casing and hang the bags to the buttons of the pocket tidy, as shown.

Strawberry pincushion [photo page 18]

1 basic sewing box (see page 6)

For 1 strawberry

10 x 15 cm novelty print cotton with a red pattern
a little synthetic filling
12 cm x 5 mm-wide green ribbon
small amount green rickrack

Cut the fabric following the pattern below, remembering to add a 1-cm margin all around to allow for the seams. Bring the straight sides together, right sides facing each other, and stitch 1 cm from the edge to make a cone, then turn right side out.

Fill this cone with stuffing, then sew a line of double-thread running stitches around the opening, 1 cm from the edge. Turn the edge in 1 cm and pull up the gathering thread tightly. Fold the ribbon in half, insert the ends of the loop into the opening and sew it closed using fine stitches, taking in all the layers of fabric.

Arrange the rickrack around the ribbon to make a calyx, and sew it on by hand using fine stitches.

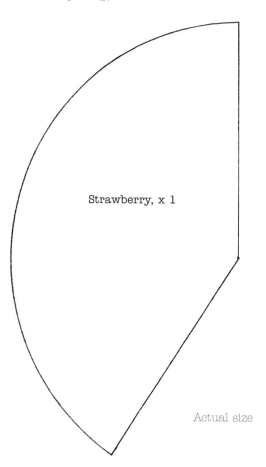

Strawberry, x 1

Actual size

Sewing basket [photo page 19]

1 basic sewing box (see page 6)

For the basket cover

7 pieces of cotton printed with different red patterns, to cut 24 rectangles,
    each 8.5 x 5.5 cm, for the patchwork top
2 rectangles thin wadding, each, 25.5 x 20 cm
2 rectangles small-checked red gingham, each 21.5 x 16 cm, for the underside of the cover
2 pieces firm scrap cardboard, each 19.5 x 14 cm
85 cm x 15 mm-wide red small-checked gingham bias binding
40 cm x 5 mm-wide green grosgrain ribbon
2 small red pompoms

For the basket insert

2 rectangles red-and-white polkadot fabric, each 28 x 18 cm, for the outer front and back, 2 rectangles,
    each19 x 18 cm, for the sides, and 1 rectangle, 24 x 15 cm, for the base
2 rectangles small-checked red gingham, each 28 x 18 cm, for the inner front and back, 2 rectangles,
    each 19 x 18 cm, for the sides, and 1 rectangle, 24 x 15 cm, for the base
2 rectangles red cotton print, each 26 x 11.5 cm, and 2 rectangles 19 x 11.5 cm, for the inner pockets
32 cm x 5 mm-wide flat elastic
4 strips red-and-white polkadot cotton, each 22 x 4 cm, for the ties
24 x 15 cm wadding
4 small white flat 2-hole buttons

Covers With right sides together and allowing 1 cm seams, sew the 24 small cotton rectangles to each other in eight rows of three along their 5.5-cm edges, then join these rows to make two 21.5 x 16 cm rectangles of four rows each. Pin each rectangle onto some thin wadding and quilt (see techniques on page 142) as indicated on the pattern on page 75, using white thread. Round the corners and trim the quilted fabric, as shown on the pattern. Trim the corners of the gingham fabric for the underside in the same way, as well as the corners of the pieces of firm cardboard (no seam allowance).

Place a patchwork cover section on a lining piece, right sides together, and stitch along the 'centre' edge (see pattern), 1 cm from the edge. With right sides together, pin and stitch one edge of the gingham bias tape along the three other sides of the patchwork cover, then turn the cover and its lining right side out. Insert a piece of cardboard between the two layers of fabric, fold the bias tape over the raw edge to the lining and sew it in place by hand using small stitches. Cut the green ribbon in half. Sew a small red pompom to one end of a piece of ribbon and attach the other end of the ribbon to the top of the cover, near the cetnre seam. Complete the second cover in the same way.

Basket insert Following the pattern on page 74, cut four pieces (front, back and two sides) from each of the polkadot fabric and the red gingham, remembering to add a 1-cm margin to allow for the seams.

Make a 1-cm double hem at the top of the four pieces of red cotton print for the pockets. Thread a piece of flat elastic through the hem of the side pockets and draw it up to reduce the width of the pockets on the width of the insert sides, and secure the ends of the elastic firmly on the wrong side.

Baste the pockets to the four gingham pieces of the inner basket insert and stitch the vertical separations on the front and back pockets, as indicated. With right sides facing each other, sew the gingham insert pieces together, stitching the side seams 1 cm from the edge. Sew the four pieces of polkadot fabric for the outer section of the insert together in the same way. Place the inner and outer inserts together, right sides facing each other, seams matching and raw edges even, and stitch all around the top, 1 cm from the edge. Turn right side out and press. Make four ties (see techniques on page 142) using the strips of red polkadot fabric and sew them to the basket insert so that they can be tied around the handle on each side.

Fuse the wadding to the gingham piece for the base of the basket insert (see techniques on page 142), then pin the base to the lower raw edge of the insert, right sides together, and stitch 1 cm from the edge. Press under 1 cm all round the polkadot base piece, then pin it in place on the wrong side of the gingham base and sew on by hand.

Place the insert inside the basket, fold the edge back over the top of the basket and secure the ties around each end of the handle. Next, sew two small white buttons on each side. Work two buttonholes on the covers to correspond with the buttons, using 2 strands of red stranded cotton, and button the covers in place.

Sewing basket

Instructions ✂ p. 73

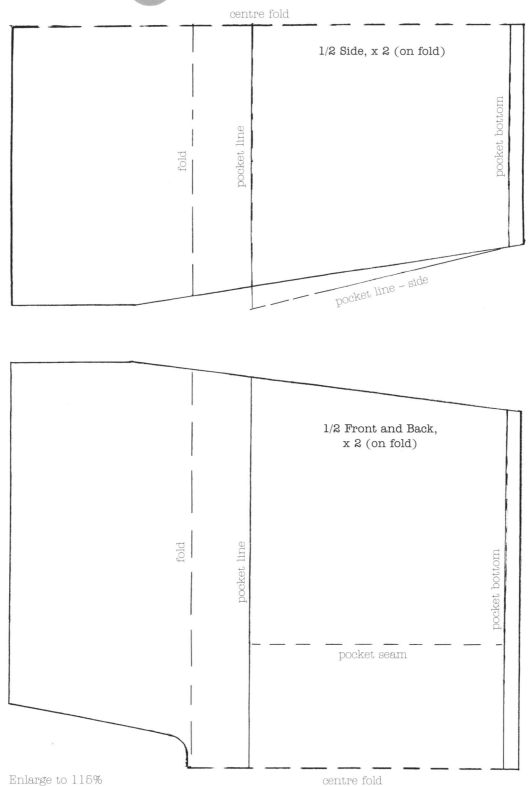

centre fold

1/2 Side, x 2 (on fold)

fold

pocket line

pocket bottom

pocket line – side

1/2 Front and Back,
x 2 (on fold)

fold

pocket line

pocket bottom

pocket seam

centre fold

Enlarge to 115%

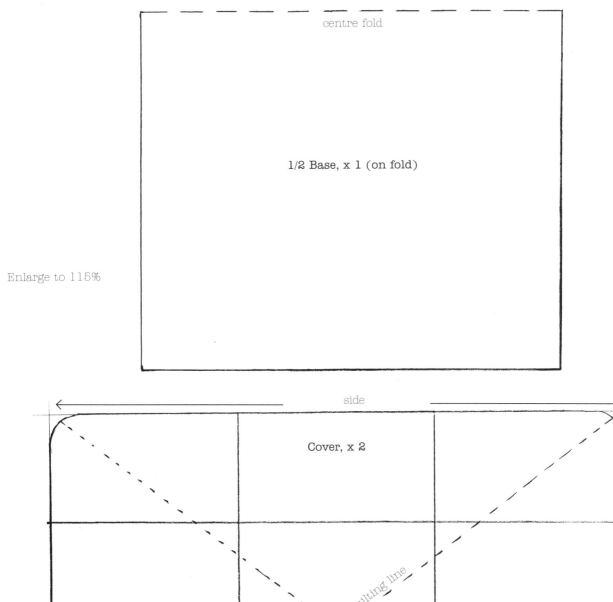

centre fold

1/2 Base, x 1 (on fold)

Enlarge to 115%

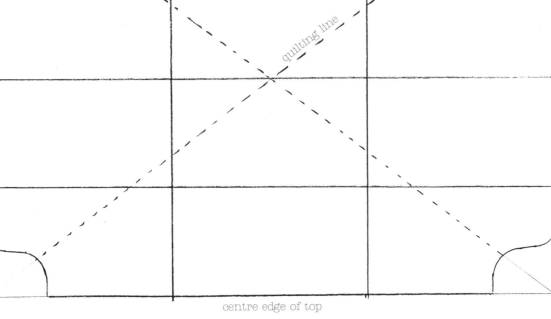

side

Cover, x 2

quilting line

centre edge of top

Square pincushions [photos pages 19 and 20-21]

Cherries

1 basic sewing box (see page 6)
small amounts red and light-green felt
12 x 12 cm red gingham, for the front
12 x 12 cm cherry-pattern fabric, for the back
42 cm green rickrack
a little synthetic filling
14 cm x 5 mm-wide satin or velvet ribbon, for the hanging loop
2 small red pompoms

Without adding seam allowance, cut out two leaves from light-green felt, following the pattern (see below), and sew them to the middle of the gingham square using large running stitches and green stranded cotton. Embroider the cherry stems using stem stitch (see techniques on page 142) and 2 strands of cotton.

Place the back and the front pieces of the pincushion on top of each other, right sides together, and stitch all around the edge, allowing a 1-cm seam and leaving an opening close to the top left corner.

Turn right side out and press. Position the rickrack all around the edge of the pincushion and stitch in place. Stuff with the synthetic filling and insert the ends of the ribbon loop into the opening. To close, sew by hand using small, fine stitches, taking in all the layers of fabric.

To finish, sew the two pompom cherries to the end of the stems.

Actual size

House

1 basic sewing box (see page 6)
fabric remnants, for the house and the sky
12 x 12 cm polkadot cotton, for the backing
14 x 14 cm thin cotton wadding
12 cm green rickrack
1 small white flat 2-hole button
1 small mushroom-shaped button
a little synthetic filling
10 cm x 10 mm-wide novelty ribbon, for the hanging loop

Cut out the different components of the house from the fabric remnants following the diagram below. Remember to add a 1-cm margin all around to allow for the seams. Join the pieces together, sewing 1 cm from the edges and following the placement diagram (below) to make a 12-cm square.

Place this patchworked square on top of the wadding, then quilt (see techniques on page 142) as shown with white thread and embroider the cross of the window in running stitch using blue stranded cotton. Sew on the rickrack, 1.5 cm from the bottom edge, and the small button at the level of the doorknob,

using red thread. Sew the mushroom button on the front, just above the rickrack 'grass'.

Place the front and back pieces of the pincushion together, right sides facing each other and raw edges matching. Stitch all around, 1 cm from the edge, leaving an opening across the top of one of the chimneys. Turn right side out, press and stuff.

Fold the ribbon in half into a loop, insert the ends into the opening and sew up using small, fine stitches, stitching through all the layers of fabric.

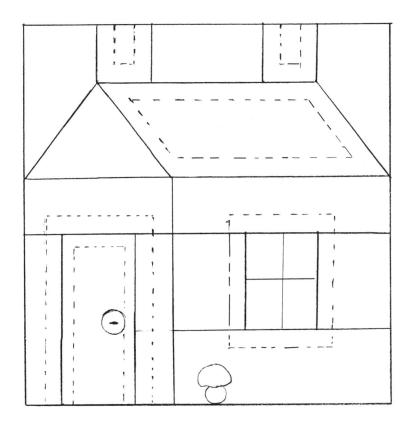

Actual size

Bunting [photo pages 22-23]

1 basic sewing box (see page 6)
48 pieces of novelty print cotton, each 25 x 30 cm
6.9 m x 20 mm-wide white cotton twill tape

Cut out 48 triangles from the pieces of novelty fabric, following the pattern opposite (remembering to add a 1-cm margin all round to allow for the seams). With right sides together, join them to each other in pairs, stitching along the long sides (the short end stays open), 1 cm from the edge.

Turn each triangle right side out, turn in 1 cm around the opening edges and press.

Press the twill tape in half lengthways. Slip the open end of each triangle between the edges of the tape and pin in place, spacing them evenly apart and positioning the first and last triangle 25 cm from the end of the tape. Baste along the length of the tape, catching each triangle in place.

Machine-sew as basted, to complete the bunting.

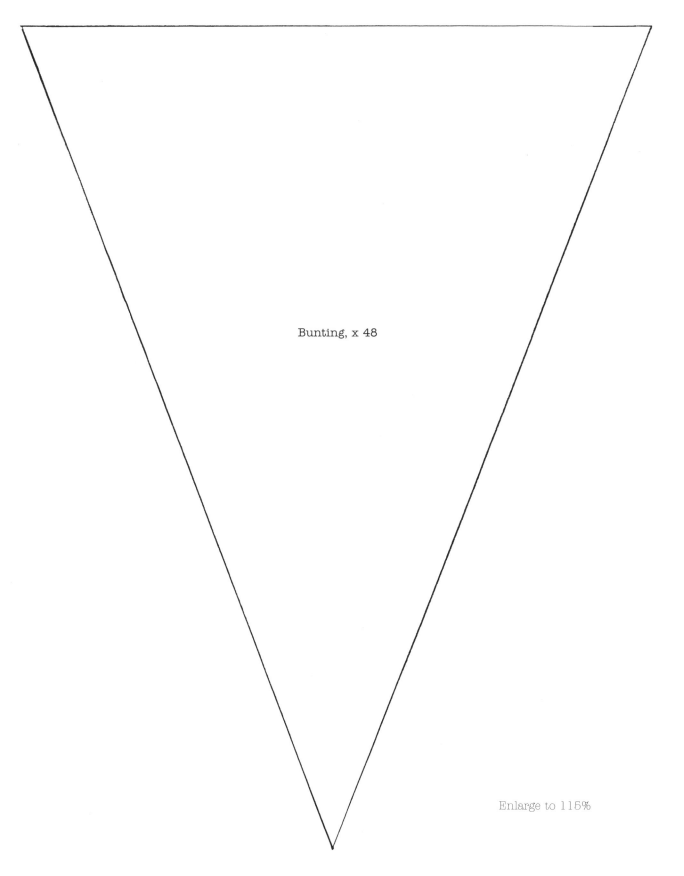

Bunting, x 48

Enlarge to 115%

Zippered purse and make-up bag [photo page 24]

Purse

1 basic sewing box (see page 6)
4 rectangles green gingham, each 11 x 5 cm
2 rectangles floral cotton, each 11 x 9 cm
2 rectangles green-and-white polkadot cotton, each 20.5 cm x 15 cm, for the front and back,
   1 rectangle, 20.5 x 7.5 cm, for the base, and 2 rectangles, each 10 x 20 cm, for the sides
60 cm pink rickrack
2 rectangles light fusible wadding, each 20.5 cm x 15 cm, 1 rectangle, 20.5 x 7.5 cm,
   and 2 rectangles, each 10 x 20 cm
2 rectangles pink-and-white striped cotton, each 28 x 8 cm, for the ruffles, and 2 strips
   with the stripes going in the opposite direction, each 22.5 x 3 cm, for the upper bands
19 cm pink zipper
2 rectangles white cotton, each 20.5 cm x 15 cm, 1 rectangle, 20.5 x 7.5 cm,
   and 2 rectangles, each 10 x 20 cm, for the lining
18 cm x 10 mm-wide pink satin ribbon

With right sides together and allowing 1-cm seams, sew a gingham rectangle to either side of a floral rectangle, along their 11-cm edges (see the diagram on page 82). Press under 1 cm on each long edge, then centre the patchwork on the polkadot rectangle for the bag front and pin in place. Cut two 15-cm pieces of pink rickrack and topstitch it in place on each side of the patchwork rectangle, sewing through all layers. Do the same thing for the back of the purse. Fuse the wadding to the wrong side of these two pieces (see techniques on page 142), as well as to the polkadot pieces for the base and sides. Trim the sides to shape, following the pattern.

To make the ruffles, fold a rectangle of striped cotton in half lengthways, right sides together, stitch the short edges 1 cm from the edge, turn right side out and press. Sew a line of gathering stitches along the raw edge and pull up to measure 18.5 cm. With raw edges matching, baste the ruffle to the top edge of the purse front. Repeat for the purse back.

Press under 1 cm on one long edge of each striped band and pin the pressed edges to the tape on each side of the zipper, centring the zipper and positioning it equidistant from each end. Topstitch in place, using a zipper foot.

With right sides together and raw edges matching, stitch the raw edge of the upper band to the upper edge of the front and back purse sections, stitching 1 cm from the edge and allowing the band to extend an equal amount beyond the purse at each end.

With right sides together, sew the lower edge of the front and back to the base, stitching 1 cm from the edge. Next, with right sides together and with the zipper open, pin the sides in place and stitch all around, stitching 1 cm from the edges. Turn right side out through the zipper.

Sew the lining pieces together, leaving the upper edge open. Press under 1 cm all around the upper edge.

Slip the lining inside the purse, wrong sides together, and hand-sew the pressed edge to the inside of the purse. To finish, tie a small ribbon to the zipper tab.

Make-up bag

1 basic sewing box (see page 6)

9 pieces of cotton fabric with different prints, for the 26 small hexagons of the front pocket

2 rectangles white cotton, each 24.5 x 16.5 cm, for the bag lining, and 1 rectangle, 24.5 x 13.5 cm, for the pocket lining

2 rectangles light wadding, each 24.5 x 16.5 cm

2 rectangles black-and-white small polkadot cotton, each 24.5 x 16.5 cm, for the outer bag

1 white zipper, 21 cm long

30 x 5 cm of one of the printed fabrics, for the hand-loop

1 small pink pompom

Using the outline on page 83, trace 26 hexagons onto the wrong side of the printed fabrics and cut out, remembering to add a 1-cm margin all around to allow for the seams. The traced line is your sewing line. With right sides together and stitching precisely along the traced lines, sew the hexagons to each other to make two rows of seven hexagons and two rows of six hexagons.

Following the traced lines, carefully sew the rows together, beginning with a row of six hexagons at the top. Place the lining on top of the assembled hexagons, right sides together, and trim the hexagons to the size of the lining. With right sides together, stitch the patchwork to the lining along the top, 1 cm from the edge, then turn right side out and press.

Baste a rectangle of wadding to the wrong side of the two polkadot rectangles for the back and front. Pin the front pocket piece to the outside of the front section, lower edges matching, trim the bottom corners to make them rounded and baste the pieces together. Round the lower corners of the back section in the same way.

Press under 1 cm on the upper edge of the back and front bag sections and pin the pressed edges to the tape on each side of the zipper, centring the zipper and positioning it equidistant from each end. Topstitch in place, using a zipper foot.

For the hand-loop, make a tie (see techniques on page 142) with the strip of printed fabric. With the right sides of the bag together, fold the tie in half and insert it between the two layers so its raw ends are level with the upper right-hand edge of the pocket. With the zipper open and allowing a 1-cm seam, stitch the sides and bottom of the bag, catching the ends of the hand-loop in the seam. Turn right side out through the zipper and press.

Place the two pieces of lining on top of each other, trim the bottom corners to make them rounded, then stitch the sides and the bottom, 1 cm from the edge. Press under 1 cm around the upper edge.

Slip the lining into the bag, wrong sides together and side seams matching, and pin the pressed edge of the lining under the zipper, on each side. Sew in place by hand, using small stitches. To finish, hang a small pompom from the pull tab of the zipper.

Purse

instructions p. 80

Placement diagram (all measurements are finished size)

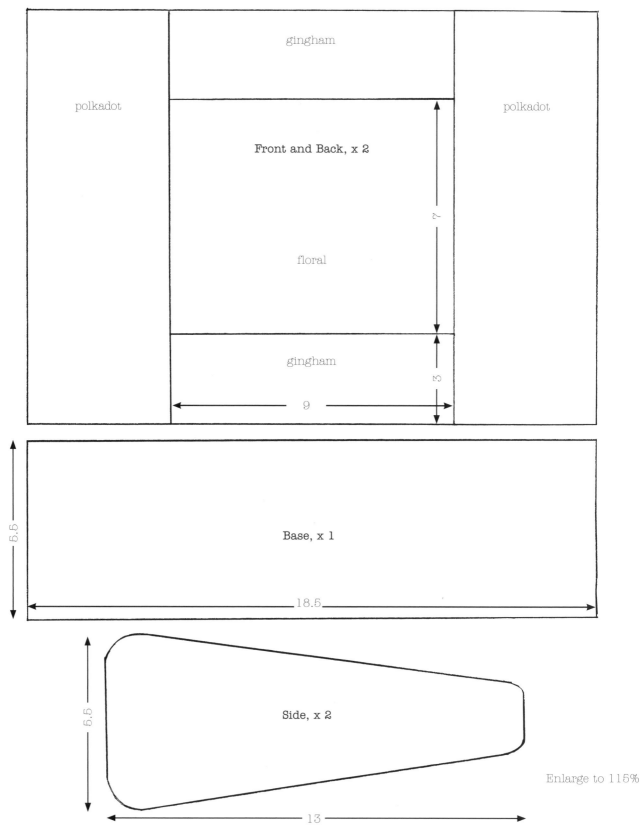

polkadot

gingham

polkadot

Front and Back, x 2

7

floral

gingham

3

9

Base, x 1

5.5

18.5

Side, x 2

5.5

13

Enlarge to 115%

Make-up bag

instructions
✂
p. 81

Hexagon,
x 26

Enlarge to 125%

hand-loop

← 11.5 →

(all measurements are finished
size)

22.5

3

← 14.5 →

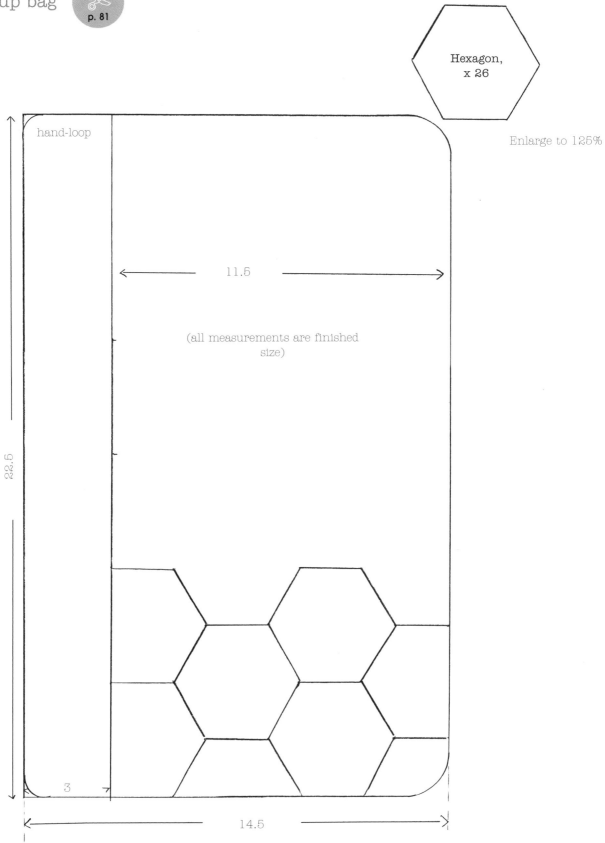

Polkadot bag [photo page 25]

1 basic sewing box (see page 6)
7 pieces of cotton fabric with different prints, to cut 7 hexagons
2 rectangles black-and-white small polkadot cotton, each 45 x 40 cm, for the outside of the bag
2 rectangles green gingham, each 45 x 40 cm, for the lining
2 rectangles green gingham, each 25 x 14 cm, for the top of the bag
2 round black ring handles

Using the outline below, trace seven hexagons onto the wrong side of the printed fabrics and cut out, remembering to add a 1-cm margin all around to allow for the seams. The traced line is your sewing line. With right sides together, sew the hexagons to each other so they form a flower, stitching along the traced lines and stopping precisely at the corners.

Using the pattern on pages 86-87, cut out the front and back pieces of the bag from polkadot fabric, remembering to add a 1-cm margin to allow for the seams. Repeat this process for the lining fabric.

Press under 1 cm all around the outer edges of the hexagon flower, pin it to the middle of the polkadot bag front and appliqué it in place by hand, using small fine stitches (see techniques on page 142).

Place the front and back bag pieces together, right sides facing each other, and stitch from the marking for the opening on one side, around the bottom of the bag to the marking for the opening on the other side, allowing a 1-cm seam. Turn right side out.

Repeat this process for the lining. With right sides together, pin the outer bag and lining to each other at the side openings and stitch, 1 cm from the edge. Push the lining back inside the bag.

Mark and baste the pleats across the top opening edges, as indicated on the pattern, taking in both layers of fabric.

Fold a rectangle of gingham in half lengthways, right sides together, and stitch the short sides, 1 cm from the edge. Turn the strip right side out. Press under 1 cm around the opening edges of the strip, then insert the top raw edge of the bag front 1 cm into this opening. Topstitch in place, stitching through all the layers of fabric. Fold the strip of gingham in half towards the lining, passing it through the loop of a ring handle, then sew the folded edge of gingham to the lining by hand, using small, firm stitches. Now repeat the process with the remaining strip of gingham to attach the second handle to the back of the bag.

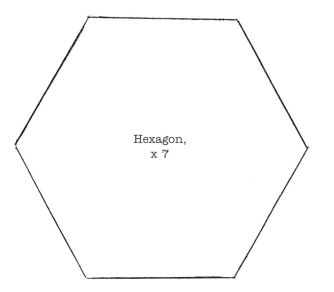

Hexagon,
x 7

Actual size

Hexagon quilted cover [photo page 26]

1 basic sewing box (see page 6)
9 pieces of cotton fabric in different prints, to cut 45 hexagons for the top
59 x 55 cm polkadot cotton, for the lining
12 small pink pompoms

Using the outline below, trace 45 hexagons onto the wrong side of the printed fabrics and cut out, remembering to add a 1-cm margin all around to allow for the seams. The traced line is your sewing line. With right sides together and stitching precisely along the traced lines, sew the hexagons to each other to make four rows of six hexagons and three rows of seven hexagons.

Following the traced lines, carefully sew the rows together, beginning and ending with a row of six hexagons. Trim two opposite sides of the patchwork to make two straight sides, remembering to leave 1-cm seam allowance on each side.

With right sides facing each other, stitch the lining and top together around the outer edges, following the traced lines of the hexagons on each end and stitching 1 cm from the edge on the straight sides. Leave an opening on one straight side. Trim the lining to 5 mm from the seam around all edges, turn right side out and press. Sew the opening closed by hand.

To finish, sew a small pink pompom to the tip of each hexagon at both ends.

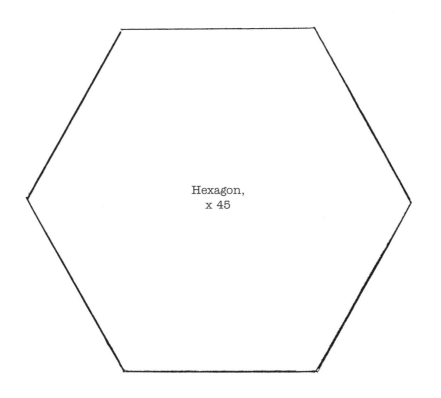

Hexagon,
x 45

Actual size

centre fold

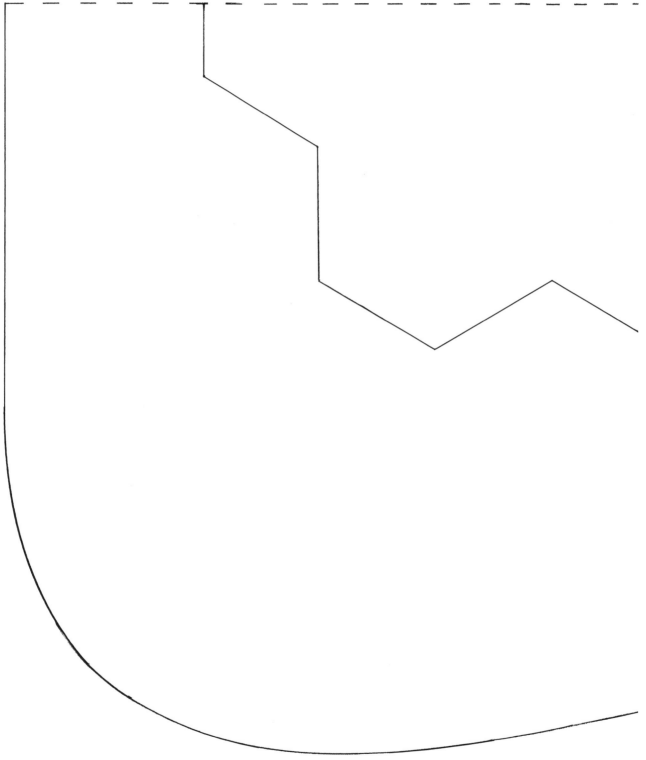

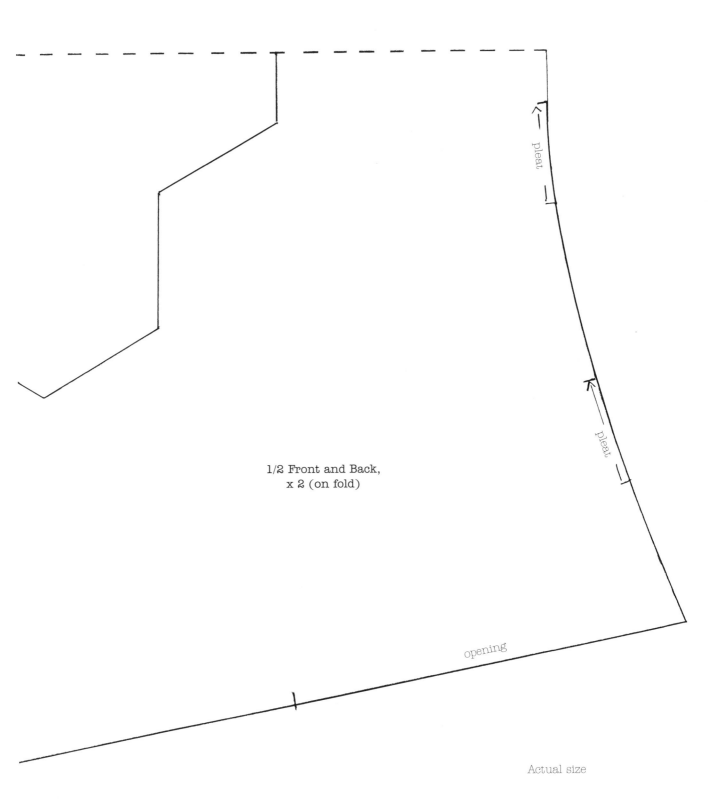

1/2 Front and Back,
x 2 (on fold)

pleat

pleat

opening

Actual size

Flowers cushion [photo page 28]

1 basic sewing box (see page 6)
double-sided fusible appliqué webbing, for the print fabrics
7 pieces of cotton fabric in different prints, for the letters
62 x 37 cm pale pink cotton, for the front
2 rectangles pale pink cotton, 24 x 37 cm, and 60 x 37 cm, for the back
4 small dark pink pompoms

Trace the letters of the word 'FLOWERS' (see pages 90-91) back-to-front onto the paper side of the double-sided appliqué webbing and cut out roughly. Fuse (see techniques on page 142) the webbing to the wrong side of the printed fabrics, then cut out accurately. Remove the backing paper from each letter and fuse the letters to the large rectangle of pink cotton.

Machine-sew around the outline of the letters in zigzag stitch. Next, embroider the outline of the F, W, R and S in blanket stitch (see techniques on page 142) using 2 strands of dark pink stranded cotton.

Press under 1 cm and then another 1 cm on one 37-cm edge of each section of the back and stitch the hem in place. Lay the two hemmed pieces out, right side up and with the hemmed edges overlapping, to make a rectangle measuring 62 x 37 cm. Place the front piece of the cushion on top of the back, right sides together. Stitch all around, 1 cm from the edge, turn right side out and press. To finish, sew a small pink pompom to each corner of the cushion.

Dreams cushion [photo page 29]

1 basic sewing box (see page 6)
10 pieces of cotton fabric in different prints, for the front of the cushion
56 cm x 40 mm-wide white lace
62 cm x 20 mm-wide white lace
2 strips of one of the printed fabrics for the front, each 50 x 6 cm, for the bows
2 rectangles pink cotton, 59 x 42 cm, and 23 x 42 cm, for the back

Following the sizes indicated on the placement diagram (see pages 92-93), cut out the rectangles and squares from the printed fabrics, adding a 1-cm margin all around each piece to allow for the seams.

With right sides together and allowing 1-cm seams, sew the squares and rectangles to each other as indicated. Construct the front in two blocks: the large square-ish shape on the left and the vertical strip to the right, then sew the two sections together for the finished front of the cushion. When you are sewing the pieces of fabric together, remember to sew the edges of the lace into the seams at the same time, as indicated on the diagram.

Embroider 'dreams' in a double row of stem stitch (see techniques on page 142) in the top right-hand rectangle, using 2 strands of dark pink stranded cotton. Embroider some stars, as shown, using large straight stitches and all 6 strands of stranded cotton.

Make two ties (see techniques on page 142) using the strips of printed fabric.

Press under 1 cm and then another 1 cm on one 42-cm edge of each section of the back and stitch the hem in place. Lay the two hemmed pieces out, right side up and with the hemmed edges overlapping, to make a rectangle measuring 62 x 42 cm. Place the front piece of the cushion on top of the back, right sides together. Stitch all around, 1 cm from the edge, turn right side out and press. Sew the ties to the right-hand edge of the cushion at evenly-spaced intervals and tie them into decorative bows.

instructions p. 88

Enlarge to 130%

Dreams cushion

Instructions ✂ p. 89

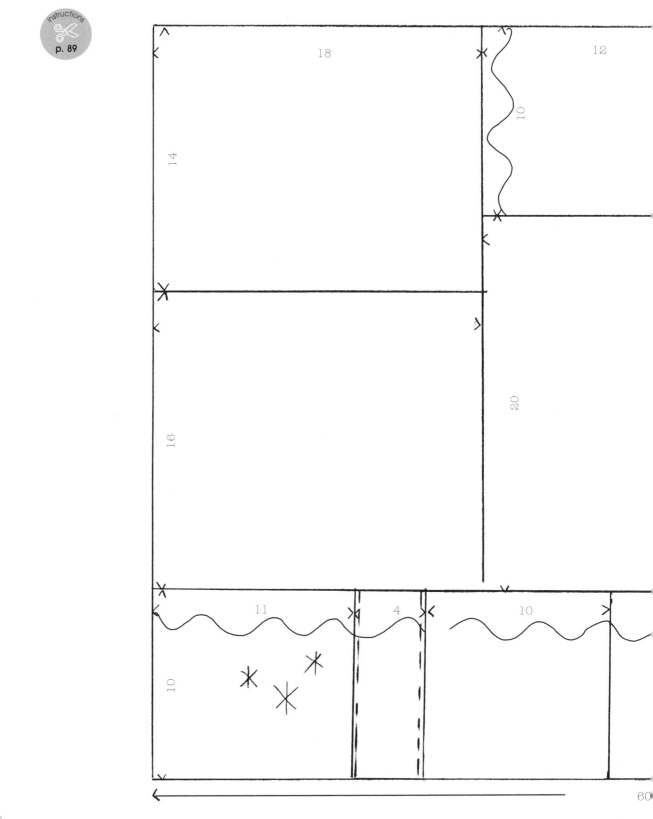

18

12

10

14

20

16

11

4

10

10

60

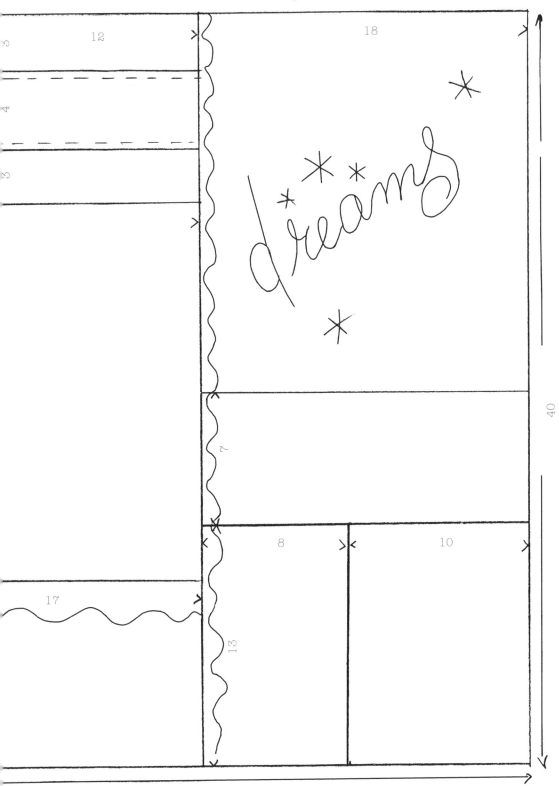

Rose tote bag [photo page 30]

1 basic sewing box (see page 6)
4 rectangles pink cotton, each 13 x 33 cm, for the front and back
2 rectangles floral cotton, each 21 x 33 cm, for the front and back
2 rectangles white cotton, each 33 x 43 cm, for the lining
2 rectangles green-and-white polkadot cotton, each 38 x 8 cm, for the upper band, and 2 strips,
  each 52 x 8 cm, for the handles
73 cm dark-pink rickrack
30 cm x 10 mm-wide dark-pink satin ribbon
1 flat white flower-shaped 2-hole button

With right sides together and allowing 1-cm seams, sew two pink panels to either side of a floral panel along their 33-cm edges for both the front and back. Following the pattern on pages 96-97, trim the bottom of each piece to make rounded corners on each side. Use one completed piece as a template to cut out the two pieces for the lining.

With right sides together and allowing 1-cm seams, sew the front and back pieces of the bag to each other around the sides and the bottom. Repeat for the two pieces of the lining, then turn the outer bag right side out and push the lining inside, wrong sides facing and seams matching. Pin the pleats, as indicated on the pattern, along the top edges of the bag, pinning through both the outside and lining layers.

Make two handles (see techniques on page 142) using the two 52 cm-long strips of polkadot cotton.

With right sides together and allowing 1-cm seams, sew the two 38-cm polkadot strips to each other along the short edges, so they form a tube. With right sides together and raw edges even, pin this tube of fabric to the top edges of the bag, matching up the side seams. Stitch as pinned, stitching 1 cm from the edge. Press under 1 cm on the remaining raw edge of the upper band, then fold the band in half over to the inside of the bag and pin the folded edge along the seam line. Insert the ends of the handles under this folded edge, as indicated on the pattern, then stitch, making sure to sew through all the layers. Pull the handles upwards, then make a second row of topstitching across the top of the polkadot band where each of the handles intersects with the band.

Topstitch the rickrack along the bottom of the polkadot band. Tie the satin ribbon into a bow and secure it to the centre front of the band by stitching on the flower button.

Bordered basket and rosette [photo page 31]

Basket

1 basic sewing box (see page 6)
2 rectangles light fusible wadding, each 63 x 15 cm
2 rectangles floral cotton, each 63 x 15 cm, for the outer border
2 rectangles pink-and-white-striped cotton, 63 x 15 cm, for the border lining, and 1 strip,
   124 x 5 cm for the upper edging

Fuse the wadding to the wrong side of the rectangles of floral fabric (see techniques on page 142). With right sides together and allowing a 1-cm seam, stitch the two rectangles to each other along one short edge. Join the two striped lining rectangles in the same way.

Using tailor's chalk and following the pattern on pages 98-99, trace the scallop outline onto the wrong side of the lining strip. The traced line will be your sewing line. Place the two strips of fabric on top of each other, right sides together, and stitch along the traced line of the scallops. Trim the fabric 5 mm from the scalloped seam. Carefully clip across the remaining seam allowance at 1-cm intervals on the curves and snip into the inner points, so that the fabric will lie flat around the curved edges when turned.

Turn right side out and press. Using pink stranded cotton, quilt by hand (see techniques on page 142) around the edge of the scallops.

Place the strip of striped fabric along the top of the scalloped band, right sides together and raw edges matching, and stitch 1 cm from the edge. Press the seam open: you now have one large strip of fabric, scalloped along the bottom. Fold in half, bringing the short edges together, right sides facing each other, and stitch 1 cm from the edge to form a tube. Press under 1 cm on the upper raw edge, then press under another 1.5 cm and topstitch the hem in place. Slip this hemmed edge over the rim of the basket, or align it with the upper edge, and attach firmly with a few stitches by hand.

Rose tote bag

Instructions p. 94

Enlarge to 140%

centre fold

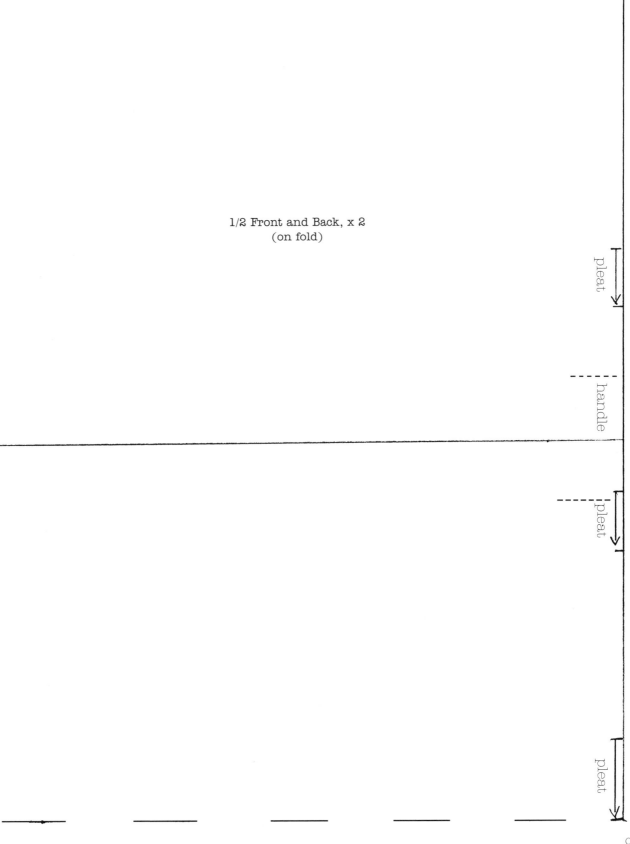

1/2 Front and Back, x 2
(on fold)

pleat

handle

pleat

pleat

Bordered basket

instructions
p. 95

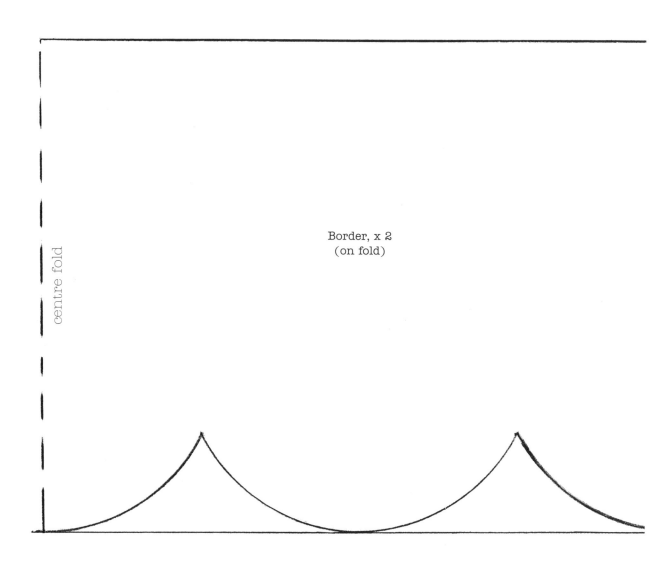

centre fold

Border, x 2
(on fold)

Actual size

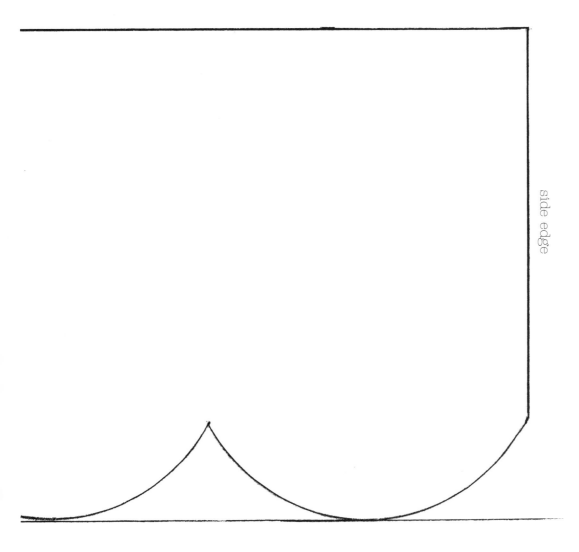

side edge

Bordered basket and rosette (continued) [photo page 31]

Rosette

1 basic sewing box (see page 6)
22 x 20 cm pin-and-white-striped cotton, for the petals
22 x 40 cm pink-and-white-polkadot cotton, for the petals, 8 x 8 cm for the backing,
   and 1 strip, 87 x 4 cm, for the ties
22 x 30 cm plain pink cotton, for the underside of the petals
small remnant floral fabric, for the centre of the flower
1 small self-cover button
5 cm dark pink rickrack

Using the patterns below, and remebering to add 1-cm seam allowance all around each piece, cut four petals from the striped fabric, eight from the polkadot fabric and 12 from the plain fabric. Cut one circle from the polkadot square. Place each plain petal on a polkadot or striped petal, right sides together, and stitch all around, 1 cm from the edge, leaving the bottom open. Turn right side out and press.

Turn in 1 cm on the raw edges of two striped petals, make a small pleat in the middle of each and sew the two petals together. Do the same thing with the two other striped petals, then sew these four petals together to make a cross. Attach the remaining petals underneath the striped petals, in the space between the petals, to make a flower.

Turn under 1 cm around the circle of polkadot fabric and sew this circle to the back of the flower to hide the assembly.

Cover a button with floral fabric and sew it to the middle of the flower, then sew a small piece of pink rickrack around it. Make a tie (see techniques on page 142) with the strip of polkadot cotton and sew the centre of the tie to the back of the flower so you can attach it wherever you want.

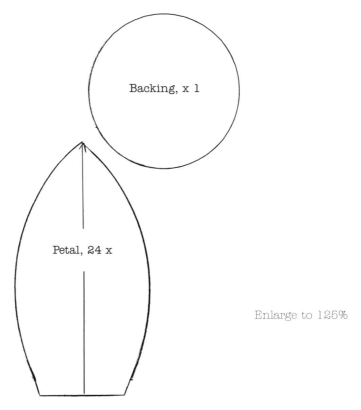

Backing, x 1

Petal, 24 x

Enlarge to 125%

Welcome decoration [photo page 32]

1 basic sewing box (see page 6)
20 x 35 cm pink gingham,
7.5 x 6.5 cm green-and-white-polkadot cotton
10 x 6.5 cm floral cotton
30 cm green rickrack
20 cm x 5 mm-wide dark pink satin ribbon
a little polyester filling

Following the pattern on page 104, cut out two complete heart shapes from the gingham, remembering to add a 1-cm margin to allow for the seams. Embroider 'Welcome' and the stars in stem stitch (see techniques on page 142) on the upper and lower sections of one heart, using two strands of pink stranded cotton. Embroider a tiny star on one of the dots of the polkadot fabric, as shown.

With right sides facing each other, sew the 6.5-cm edges of the polkadot and floral rectangles together to make a strip. Press under 5 mm on the top and bottom raw edges of the strip, then pin it across the front heart, as shown, tucking the edge of a piece of rickrack under each edge of the strip. Sew the pinned edges in place, using large running stitches and pink stranded cotton, catching the rickrack in the seam. Trim the edge of the strip to match the heart outline.

Place the back and front hearts together, right sides facing each other, and insert the pink ribbon, folded in two, between the two layers, with its ends just reaching the dent in the top of the heart.

Stitch all around the heart, 1 cm from the edge, securing the raw ends of the ribbon loop in the seam, and leaving an opening in one side, for turning.

Turn right side out, press, fill with polyester filling, then sew the opening closed by hand.

Home sweet home decoration [photo page 33]

1 basic sewing box (see page 6)
15 x 6 cm pink gingham, for the roof
15 x 8.5 cm white cotton with small flowers, for the house front
15 x 4 cm floral fabric, for the garden
15 x 14.5 cm pink polkadot cotton, for the backing
pink-patterned fabric remnants, for the 'H', the door and the window
1 small white flat 2-hole button
15 cm green rickrack
22 cm x 5 mm-wide pale-pink satin ribbon
a little polyester filling

Using the pattern on page 104 as a guide and allowing 1-cm seams, sew the different fabrics for the roof, house front and garden together along their 15-cm edges, to make a rectangle measuring 15 x 14.5 cm. Cut out the window, door and 'H' (do not add seam allowance) and machine-zigzag them in place on the house front. Embroider the outline of the H in blanket stitch (see techniques on page 142), using two strands of pink cotton. Embroider the cross of the window and the star using large straight stitches. Sew on a white button for the door knob.

Embroider 'home' in stem stitch (see techniques on page 142), using two strands of pink stranded cotton and stitch the rickrack just above the floral fabric 'garden'.

Pin the front and back pieces of the house together, right sides facing each other. With tailor's chalk, trace and then cut away the slope of the roof, as indicated, leaving a 1-cm margin. Fold the ribbon in half into a loop and insert it between the two layers, with the raw ends at the centre of the top of the roof.

Allowing a 1-cm seam, stitch all around, securing the ends of the ribbon in the seam and leaving an opening in the bottom edge for turning.

Turn right side out, press, stuff with polyester filling, then sew the opening closed by hand.

Shopping bags [photo page 34]

1 basic sewing box (see page 6)
4 rectangles natural linen, each 38 x 8 cm, for the front and back, 1 rectangle, 88 x 12 cm, for the gusset,
  2 rectangles, each 48 x 6 cm, for the upper lining, and 2 rectangles, each 14 x 3.5 cm, for the handle casings
6 strips polkadot cotton in 3 different colours, each 38 x 4 cm, for the front and back
4 strips floral cotton in 2 different colours, each 38 x 6 cm, for the front and back
50 cm x 90 cm-wide x 5 mm-thick fusible wadding
1.9 m natural linen piping
40 cm x 90 cm-wide black gingham, for the lining
2 x 12 cm-wide bamboo D-handles
2 x 15 cm-long threadbars and 4 screws
1 large press-stud or magnetic bag snap
2 small transparent press-studs
60 cm x 20 mm-wide black twill tape

With right sides facing each other and allowing 1-cm seams, sew the rectangles of linen and cotton together along their 38-cm edges, in the order indicated on the diagram on page 107, to make the patchwork back and front of the bag. Round off the lower corners, as shown. Following the diagram on page 106, trim the long strip of natural linen into the shape of the gusset.

From wadding, cut a back, a front and a gusset, using the fabric pieces as a template, then fuse them to the wrong side of the appropriate fabric sections (see techniques on page 142).

Baste some piping around the sides and bottom of the front piece, 1 cm from the edge, and do the same thing for the back of the bag. Next, with right sides together, baste the gusset in place between the front and back pieces and stitch along the 1-cm basting line, sandwiching the piping in the seam. Turn right side out and press.

Turn under 1 cm on the short edges of the linen strips for the handle casings, then fold each strip in half lengthways, wrong sides together. With raw edges even, centre these strips along the top edge of the bag, one at the front and one at the back, and pin in place.

Place the two rectangles of natural linen for the upper lining together, right sides facing each other, and stitch the short sides 1 cm from the edge, to form

a tube. With right sides together and raw edges even, pin this tube around the top of the bag, and stitch all around, 1 cm from the edge, sewing through all the layers, then fold the upper lining over to the inside of the bag and press.

From the gingham for the bag lining, cut a gusset lining, following the diagram on page 106 (remembering to add 1-cm seam allowance to the measurements), as well as two pieces, each measuring 38 x 24 cm, for the back and the front. Assemble the lining as for the outside of the bag, but without the piping, and leaving an opening in one bottom seam for turning. With right sides together, pin the top of the gingham lining to the raw edge of the linen upper lining and stitch, 1 cm from the edge. Turn right side out through the opening in the lining, then stitch the opening closed by hand. Push the lining back inside the bag.

Attach the handles to the bag following the manufacturer's instructions.

Sew a large press-stud or magnetic snap to the upper lining on the inside, between the handles, so you can close the bag. Sew a small transparent press-stud to the outside of the bag at the top of each side, so that you can adjust the width of the bag, if desired. Sew the black twill tape onto the bag, near one of the handles, and tie into a decorative bow.

Small quilted bag [photos pages 35 and 36]

1 basic sewing box (see page 6)
20 x 15 cm natural linen for the base, and 24 x 8 cm, for the handle
46.5 x 15 cm sky-blue-and-white polkadot cotton, for the bag lining, and 20 x 15 cm, for the base lining
8 pieces of cotton fabric in different prints, to cut 30 squares, each 6.5 cm, for the outside of the bag
46.5 x 15 cm thick fusible wadding, for the bag, 20 x 15 cm, for the base, and 24 x 8 cm, for the handle
3 x 9 cm-diameter circles, cut from fabric scraps, for the yo-yos
10 cm x 20 mm-wide black twill tape

Using the pattern below, cut one base for the bag from the 20 x 15 cm piece of linen, adding a 1-cm margin to allow for the seams. Cut a lining base from the polkadot fabric, cutting it 5 mm smaller all round than the linen.

With right sides together and allowing 1-cm seams, sew the squares to each other in three rows of ten, pressing all the seam allowances in each row in alternate directions. Sew the rows together to make a large patchwork rectangle. Fuse some thick wadding to the wrong side of this rectangle and also to the linen base of the bag (see techniques on page 142).

Fold the patchwork rectangle in half, bringing the short edges together, right sides facing each other, and stitch 1 cm from the short edge to make a tube. With right sides together, pin this tube to the linen base, and stitch all around, 1 cm from the edge. Sew the lining in the same way, leaving an opening in the side seam so you can turn it inside out.

Fuse some wadding to the wrong side of the 24 x 8 cm linen rectangle, then fold it in two lengthways, right sides together. Stitch along the length, 1 cm from the edge, turn right side out and press, positioning the seam down the middle.

With right sides together and raw edges even, pin the lining to the outer bag around the top edge, inserting the handle between the two layers so that its two ends will be sewn into the seam. Stitch all around, 1 cm from the edge, sewing through all the layers, and turn right side out through the opening in the lining. Sew the opening closed by hand and tuck the lining back inside the bag.

Sew a line of running stitch 1.5 cm inside the edge around a fabric circle to make a gathering thread, turn in 1.5 cm on the edge and pull up the gathering thread to make a yo-yo 3 cm in diameter. Make another two other yo-yos in the same way, then sew them onto the outside of the bag, as shown, catching a twill-tape bow in place at the same time.

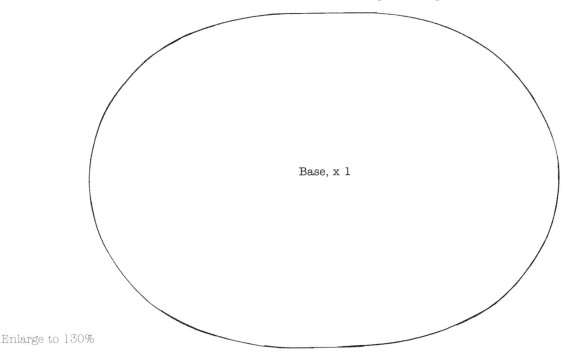

Base, x 1

Enlarge to 130%

Welcome

instructions
p. 101

Enlarge to 125%

Home sweet home

instructions
p. 101

Enlarge to 125%

Diary cover [photo page 37]

1 basic sewing box (see page 6)
1 notebook, A5 format, 14.8 x 21 cm
2 rectangles white cotton with polkadots, each 47 x 8 cm, for the outside
47 x 11.5 cm floral cotton, for the outside
47 x 23.5 cm white cotton, for the lining
90 cm x 5 mm-wide red cotton or grosgrain ribbon
9 cm-diameter circle of red polkadot cotton, for the yo-yo
1 small white button

With right sides facing each other and allowing 1-cm seams, sew the rectangles of polkadot and floral cotton togther along their 47-cm edges, to make a large rectangle measuring 47 x 23.5 cm, for the outside of the cover. Lay it on the lining, right sides together and raw edges matching.

Stitch all around, 1 cm from the edge, leaving an opening on one side. Turn right side out, press and sew the opening closed by hand.

To make the flaps that will hold the notebook, fold in each short side 6 cm towards the lining, then topstich at the top and bottom, 1 mm from the edge.

Sew one of the ends of the red ribbon to the front of the notebook cover, in the middle and again, 3.5 cm from the edge.

Sew a line of running stitch all around the fabric circle, 1.5 cm from the edge, to make a gathering thread. Fold the edge in 1.5 cm and pull up the thread to make a yo-yo, 3 cm in diameter. Attach this yo-yo to the small white button, and sew both, a little loosely, to the end of the red ribbon that is attached to the cover. To close and secure the notebook, you just need to wrap the long end of the ribbon a few times around the notebook, then wrap it around the yo-yo.

Shopping bags

Instructions
p. 102

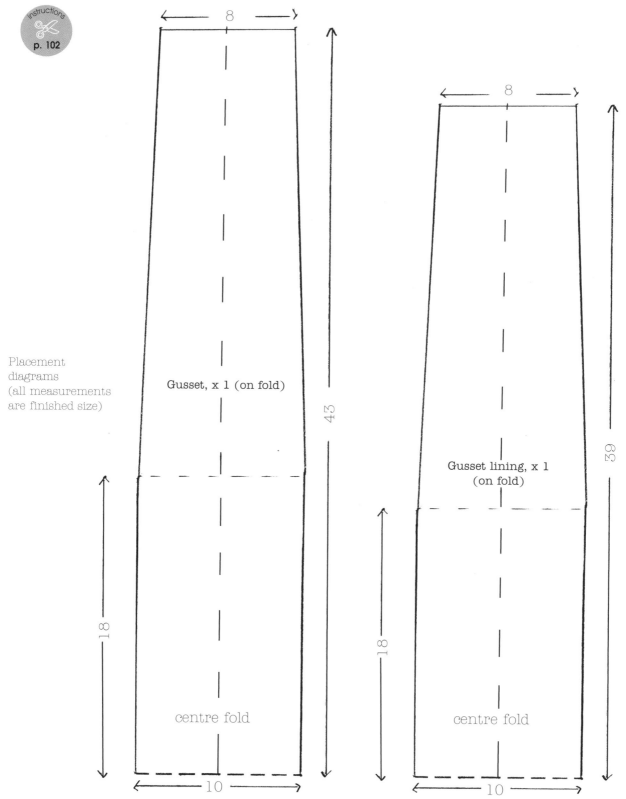

Placement
diagrams
(all measurements
are finished size)

Gusset, x 1 (on fold)

8

43

18

centre fold

10

Gusset lining, x 1
(on fold)

8

39

18

centre fold

10

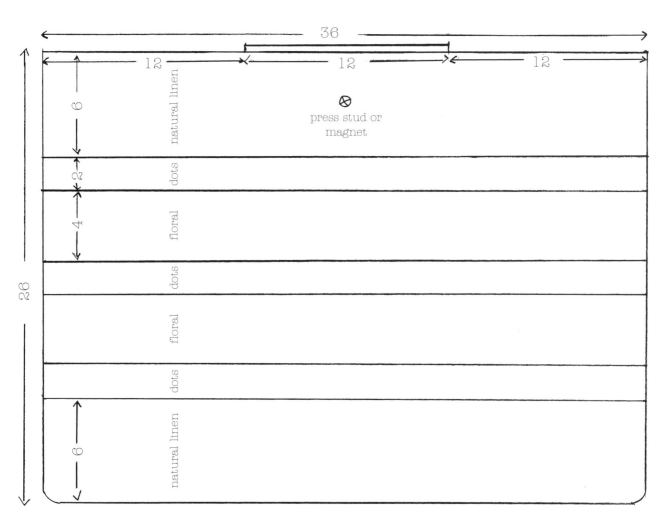

36

12

12

12

6

natural linen

⊗

press stud or
magnet

2

dots

4

floral

dots

floral

dots

26

6

natural linen

Front and Back, x 2
(all measurements are finished size)

Tissue case [photo page 39]

1 basic sewing box (see page 6)
15.5 x 11 cm natural linen, for the back
2 rectangles sky-blue-and-white polkadot cotton, each 15.5 x 6 cm, for the front
50 cm x 5 mm-wide red cotton ribbon
9 cm-diameter circle of floral cotton, for the yo-yo

Place the two rectangles of polkadot fabric together, right sides facing each other, and make a 3.5 cm line of stitching at the top and bottom of one long side, 5 mm from the edge, leaving an 8.5 cm opening in the middle. Press the seam open along the length, including the opening edges. Baste a piece of red ribbon along each side of the opening, then stitch the ribbon in place as basted.

Place the piece of linen backing on the polkadot front, right sides together and raw edges matching, then stitch all around, allowing a 1-cm seam. Turn right side out and press.

Sew a line of running stitch all around the fabric circle, 1.5 cm from the edge, to make a gathering thread. Fold the edge in 1.5 cm and pull up the thread to make a yo-yo, 3 cm in diameter.

Tie the remaining red ribbon into a decorative bow and sew it to the top of the case at one end of the opening, then stitch the yo-yo on top.

Mobile phone pouch [photo page 39]

1 basic sewing box (see page 6)
24.5 x 10.5 cm floral cotton, for the outside
24.5 x 10.5 cm light fusible wadding, and 1 rectangle, 19 x 5 cm
24.5 x 10.5 cm white cotton, for the lining
5 cm black Velcro
21 x 7 cm red-and-white polkadot cotton, for the flap, and 88 x 4 cm, for the strap
20 cm x 5 mm-wide red cotton ribbon
15 cm x 5 mm-wide black cotton ribbon
small piece of 10 mm-wide numbered selvedge

Fuse a piece of light wadding to the wrong side of the floral fabric (see techniques on page 142), then place the lining and the fused fabric together, right sides facing each other. Stitch all around, 1 cm from the edge, leaving a 5-cm opening along one of the short sides, then turn right side out and press. Sew one section of Velcro lengthways to the right side of the rectangle, 2 cm from the finished short edge.

Centre the remaining piece of light wadding on the wrong side of the polkadot fabric and fuse in place. Sew the remaining section of Velcro lengthways to the right side of the fabric, 4.5 cm from the edge of one of the short sides. Fold the polkadot fabric in half, bringing the two short edges together, so that the Velcro is on the inside. Stitch the sides, 1 cm from the edge, rounding the bottom corners. Turn this flap right side out and press.

Make a tie (see techniques on page 142) from the long strip of polkadot fabric.

Place the assembled piece for the case in front of you, the white lining side up. Fold the tie in half and insert the two ends, one on top of the other, into the opening at the top. Insert the raw edge of the flap as well, Velcro facing you. Stitch, sewing through all the layers.

Fold the cover in half across the middle, and topstitch the sides, 1 mm from the edge. Tie the black ribbon into a small bow and sew it to the outside of the flap, as well as a small piece of numbered selvedge, for decoration.

Placemat [photo page 40]

1 basic sewing box (see page 6)
20 x 20 cm double-sided fusible appliqué webbing
4 squares of different fancy print cottons, each 8 x 8 cm, for the flowers
  52 x 39 cm linen, for the top
2 strips navy blue polkadot cotton ribbon, each 52 cm x 20 mm-wide, and 2 pieces,
  each 39 cm x 20 mm-wide
52 x 39 cm pink polkadot cotton, for the backing

Using the patterns opposite and below, trace the flower shapes onto the appliqué webbing and cut out roughly, a little outside the traced line. Fuse the appliqué webbing to the wrong side of the flower fabrics (see techniques on page 142), then cut out the flowers accurately along the traced outlines.

Fuse the flowers to the linen rectangle, as shown, then embroider their outline in blanket stitch (see techniques on page 142), using pink and light-blue stranded cotton. Embroider the flower centres and the leaves using large straight stitches and running stitch in navy blue and red stranded cotton.

Pin the pieces of ribbon around the edges of the mat and topstitch in place along the inner edges.

Place the top mat and backing together, right sides facing each other and raw edges matching, and stitch all around, 1 cm from the edge, leaving an opening.

Turn right side out, press and sew the opening neatly closed by hand.

Actual size

lower left corner, x 1

upper right corner, x 1

Actual size

Flower tea cosy [photo page 41]

1 basic sewing box (see page 6)
2 rectangles pink gingham, each 30 x 25 cm, for the outside
2 rectangles white cotton, each 30 x 25 cm, for the lining
20 x 20 cm double-sided fusible appliqué webbing
3 scraps of cotton fabric in different prints, for the flowers
2 rectangles thin cotton wadding, each 30 x 25 cm
1 small white button
54 x 6 cm navy-and-white polkadot cotton, and 1 strip, 8 x 2 cm

Following the pattern on pages 114-115 and remembering to add a 1-cm margin for the seams, cut a front and back from gingham for the outside of the tea cosy, and a front and back from white cotton for the lining. Trace the flower shapes onto the appliqué webbing and cut out roughly, a little outside the traced line. Fuse the appliqué webbing to the wrong side of the flower fabrics (see techniques on page 142), then cut out the flowers accurately along the traced outlines.

Fuse the flowers in place on the front of the tea cosy. Baste the front and back of the tea cosy to the pieces of cotton wadding. Sew a button to the centre of the first flower, then embroider the centres of the two others using red and navy blue stranded cotton, the stem and leaves in navy blue large running stitches and the outline of the flowers with large blanket stitch (see techniques on page 142) in pink. Next, trim the wadding even with the fabric edge on front and back.

Place the two lining pieces together, right sides facing each other, and stitch around the rounded section, 1 cm from the edge. Finish the edges of the small strip of polkadot fabric with machine-zigzag.

Place the two outer tea cosy pieces together, right sides facing each other. Fold the small polkadot strip into a loop and insert it at the top, between the two layers. Stitch around the rounded section, 1 cm from the edge, securing the ends of the loop in the seam. To reduce bulk, trim the seam allowance of the wadding back to the stitching line. Turn right side out and insert the lining into the outer cosy, wrong sides together and seams matching.

With right sides together, pin the long strip of polkadot fabric all around the opening, folding in the ends neatly. Stitch 1 cm from the edge, sewing through all layers. Fold the fabric over towards the wrong side, turn under 1 cm on the raw edge and hand-sew in place using blind running stitches.

Bird tea cosy [photo page 42]

1 basic sewing box (see page 6)
6 pieces of cotton fabric in different prints, to cut 22 triangles, each about 7 cm high
2 rectangles pink-and-white-striped cotton, each 35 x 20 cm, for the outside
10 x 10 cm pink-and-white polkadot fabric, for the bird
   fabric remnants, for the flower and leaves
2 rectangles thin cotton wadding, each 40 x 31.5 cm
1 small white 4-hole button and 1 other button, a little larger
20 cm beige rickrack
2 rectangles white cotton, each 35 x 25 cm, for the lining
62 x 6 cm strip navy blue polkadot fabric, for the lower band, and 1 strip,
   25 x 4 cm, for the bow on top

Cut out 22 isosceles triangles from the different fabrics, each with a base of 8 cm and sides of 7.5 cm. Allowing 1-cm seams, sew them together to make two rows of 11 triangles, as shown on the pattern, on pages 116-117.

Using the pattern, cut the upper part of the tea cosy twice from the striped fabric, remembering to add a 1-cm margin to allow for the seams. With right sides together, centre and sew a row of triangles to the straight edge of each striped upper section, stitching 1 cm from the edges. (The triangles will extend at each end. Use the pattern to trim them to size, remembering the seam allowance.) Cut the bird shape from the pink polkadot fabric, following the pattern and adding a 5 mm margin all around. Turn under 5 mm around the edge and press. Cut out two flower shapes from fabric remnants, adding a 1-cm margin all round. With right sides facing each other and allowing a 1-cm seam, stitch the flowers together around the outer edge, leaving a small opening. Clip across the seam allowance on the curves, turn right side out, press and sew the opening closed. Cut out the leaves without adding any margin. Machine-zigzag stitch around each leaf.

Centre the front side of the tea cosy, right side up, on top of a piece of wadding. Using the pattern as a guide, position the different elements of the design on top and quilt (see techniques on page 142) them in place, working round the outline of the bird and leaves with running stitch. Hold the flower in position by sewing a button to the centre, leaving the petals free, then work a line of running stitch around the button. Sew the remaining button in place, as shown. Outline-quilt around each of the triangles, about 5 mm from the seams. Stitch on the piece of rickrack and embroider the wing and the feet of the bird in stem stitch (see techniques on page 142). Work a French knot for the eye. Next, trim the wadding 1 cm inside the fabric. Centre the back of the tea cosy, right side up, on the remaining piece of wadding and outline-quilt around the triangles, as for the front. Baste around the edge of the fabric, then trim the wadding to size.

Using the quilted front as a template, cut out two pieces from the white cotton, for the lining. Place these two pieces together, right sides facing each other, and sew around the outer edge, 1 cm from the edge, leaving the lower edge open. Repeat for the two outer pieces. Trim the wadding back to the stitching to reduce bulk. Insert the lining into the outer cosy, wrong sides together and matching side seams.

With right sides together, pin the polkadot band all around the opening, and stitch 1 cm from the edge, sewing through all layers and folding in the raw edges neatly at each end. Fold the strip over to the wrong side, press under 1 cm on the raw edge and sew in place using small invisible stitches.

To finish, make a tie (see techniques on page 142) with the strip of polkadot fabric, tie it into a small bow and sew it to the top of the tea cosy.

Flower tea cosy

instructions
p. 112

tie

Enlarge to 110%

tie

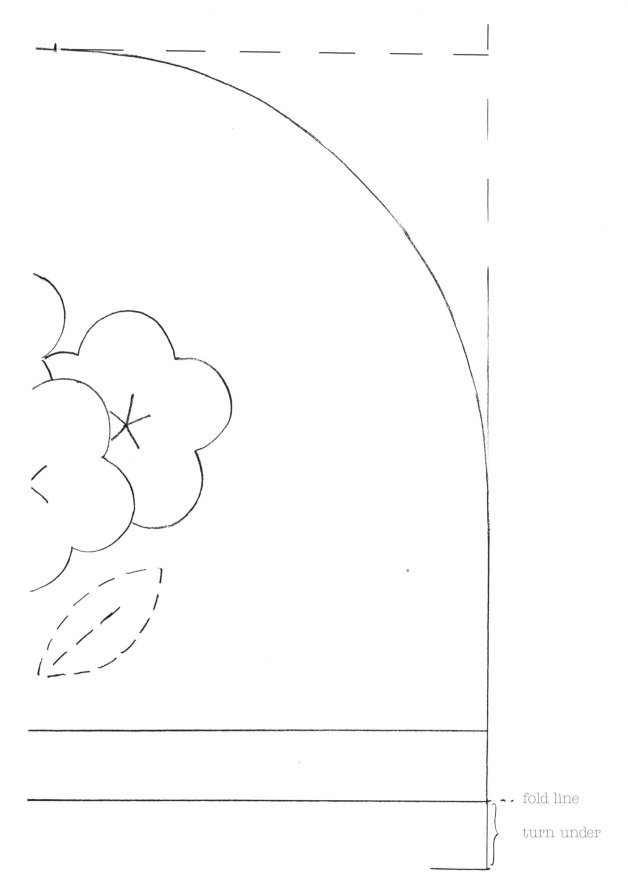

fold line

turn under

115

Bird tea cosy

Instructions
✂
p. 113

Enlarge to 120%

fold line

turn under

117

Kitchen pocket wall-hanging [photo page 43]

1 basic sewing box (see page 6)

60 cm x 90 cm-wide light fusible wadding

48 x 62 cm linen, for the front

3 rectangles teatowel fabric, each 40 x 18 cm, for the pockets

small amount double-sided fusible appliqué webbing

small amounts of 5 different fabrics, for the appliqué shapes

22.5 x 16 cm striped cotton, for the middle pocket

2.3 m navy-blue rickrack

15 cm pink rickrack

1 self-cover button, 3 small white flat buttons, and 1 flat red button

48 x 62 cm navy-and-white polkadot cotton, for the back, 3 rectangles, each 40 x 18 cm,
  for the pockets linings,

1 rectangle, 48 x 7 cm, for the top of the hanging, and 1 strip, 64 x 4 cm, for the strap

48 cm x 20 mm-wide twill tape, for the casing on the back

57 x cm x 10 mm-diameter wooden dowel

2 x 9 cm-diameter circles of cotton, for the yo-yos

1 brooch pin

3 transparent press-studs

Fuse the wadding to the wrong side of the three teatowel rectangles and the linen fabric (see techniques on page 142).

Trace the appliqué shapes (opposite) onto the paper side of some appliqué webbing and cut out roughly just outside the traced line. Fuse the webbing onto the wrong side of your fabric remnants, then cut out accurately on the traced line. Machine-zigzag around the edges of the shapes.

Press a 1-cm double hem on one long side of the striped rectangle, then topstitch a little navy rickrack along the hem, on the inside, as shown. Remove the backing paper and fuse the teapot motif to the centre of the fabric, then sew on a little pink rickrack and a button covered (see techniques on page 142) with the same fabric as the teapot. Press under 1 cm on the remaining three raw edges and topstitch the pocket onto a rectangle of teatowel fabric for the middle pocket.

Fuse the appliqué motifs to the teatowel rectangles for the top and bottom pockets, then sew on the pieces of rickrack and the buttons, as shown. Place each of the three pieces of tea towel on top of their polkadot lining rectangles, right sides together, and stitch all around, 1 cm from the edge, leaving a small opening at the bottom. Turn right side out, turn in 1 cm on each of the openings and press.

Pin the pockets to the linen rectangle, positioning the first one 4 cm from the bottom and leaving a 1.5-cm space between each. Topstitch the pockets in place around the side and bottom edges, stitching 1 mm from the edge. Next, lay the polkadot lining on top of the pockets, right sides together, and stitch around the sides and bottom, 1 cm from the edge. Turn right side out and press. Stitch blue ricrack all around the border, 2 cm from the edges, then turn under 1 cm on both raw edges of the top opening and press to mark the folds.

Make a 1 cm hem on the two short ends of the rectangle of polkadot fabric, then fold this fabric in two lengthways, wrong sides together, insert the raw edges into the top of the kitchen hanging and topstitch along the top, making sure to sew through all the layers of fabric.

Stitch the twill tape to the back of the hanging, at the top of the linen, to make a casing, and insert the rod. Make a tie (see techniques on page 142) from the long strip of polkadot fabric, then fold over 3 cm on each end of the strap and stitch to form a loop. Pass the ends of the rod through these loops, then make a few stitches by hand at the top of the polkadot fabric to catch the strap to the border and stop it sagging.

To make the yo-yos, sew a line of running stitch all around each fabric circle, 1.5 cm from the edge, to make a gathering thread. Fold the edge in 1.5 cm and pull up the thread to make two yo-yos, each 3 cm in diameter. Sew a small white button to the centre of each yo-yo. Sew one yo-yo to the brooch pin, and the other on top of a press-stud, positioned so that it closes one of the pockets. Sew on the two other press-studs according to how you want to use the hanging.

Enlarge to 120%

Recipe book cover [photo page 44]

1 basic sewing box (see page 6)
62 x 22.5 cm navy-and-white polkadot cotton, for the outside
62 x 22.5 cm blue-and-white-striped cotton, for the inside
small remnant floral fabric
small amount double-sided fusible appliqué webbing
20 x 20cm recipe notebook

Sketch your initial letter by hand or trace a letter in a simple strong font (from your computer or a magazine) and enlarge it to about 5-6 cm high. Trace the letter, back to front, onto the appliqué webbing and cut out roughly, a little outside the traced line. Fuse (see techniques on page 142) the appliqué webbing to the wrong side of the floral fabric, then cut out the letter accurately along the traced outline.

Remove the backing paper and machine-zigzag around the edge of the letter in a contrast colour, then fuse it to the polkadot fabric, centring it on one half of the fabric.

Place the polkadot fabric and striped lining together, right sides facing each other, and stitch all around, 1 cm from the edge, leaving an opening. Turn right side out, press and sew the opening closed by hand.

Next, turn in a 10-cm flap at each end of this strip and topstitch the top and bottom of the flaps, 1 mm from the edge. Insert your book into the cover.

Little pots [photo page 45]

Flowers

1 basic sewing box (see page 6)
2 rectangles light fusible wadding, each 28 x 7 cm, and 2 circles, each 8.5 cm in diameter
30 x 9 cm navy-and-white polkadot cotton, 1 circle, 10.5 cm in diameter, for the lining,
    and 1 strip, 50 x 4 cm, for the tie
30 x 9 cm floral cotton, and 1 circle, 10.5 cm in diameter, for the outside
28 cm navy-blue rickrack

Fuse (see techniques on page 142) the wadding to the centre of the wrong side of the two fabric circles and the two large rectangles.

With right sides facing each other and allowing a 1-cm seam, stitch the short edges of the floral rectangle together, forming a tube. Repeat this process for the polkadot rectangle, but leave an opening in the middle of the seam. With right sides together, stitch the corresponding circular base in place on each tube, allowing a 1-cm seam.

Baste the rickrack to the right side of the upper edge of the floral pot, positioning it so that it will extend above the seam when it is stitched. Slip one pot inside the other, right sides together, then stitch around the upper edge, 1 cm from the edge, catching the rickrack in the seam. Turn right side out through the side opening and press. Sew the opening closed by hand, then push the polkadot fabric down inside the outer pot. Make a tie (see techniques on page 142) from the long strip of polkadot fabric and tie it around the finished pot.

Gingham

1 basic sewing box (see page 6)
2 rectangles light fusible wadding, each 28 x 7 cm, and 2 circles, each 8.5 cm in diameter
30 x 9 cm navy-and-white polkadot cotton, and 1 circle, 10.5 cm in diameter, for the lining
30 x 9 cm pink gingham, and 1 circle, 10.5 cm in diameter, for the outside
small piece of floral fabric
30 cm pink rickrack

Fuse (see techniques on page 142) the wadding to the centre of the wrong side of the two fabric circles and the two large rectangles.

Cut a simple shape from the floral fabric scrap, then sew it to the middle of the gingham rectangle with blanket stitch (see techniques on page 142), using pink stranded cotton.

With right sides facing each other and allowing a 1-cm seam, stitch the short edges of the gingham rectangle together, forming a tube. Repeat this process for the polkadot rectangle, but leave an opening in the middle of the seam. With right sides together, stitch the corresponding circular base in place on each tube, allowing a 1-cm seam.

Slip one pot inside the other, right sides together, then stitch around the upper edge, 1 cm from the edge. Turn right side out through the side opening and press. Sew the opening closed by hand, then push the polkadot fabric down inside the outer pot. To finish, sew some rickrack around the top edge by hand.

Striped apron [photo page 46]

1 basic sewing box (see page 6)
1 m x 110 cm-wide blue-and-white-striped canvas
57 x 6 cm strip pink-and-white polkadot cotton, for the neck loop, and 2 strips,
  each 86 x 6 cm, for the ties
18 x 15 cm navy-blue-and-white polkadot cotton, for the small pocket, and 1 rectangle,
  65 cm x 15 mm-wide navy blue rickrack
32 x 25 cm floral cotton, for the pocket
1 flat white 4-hole button

Following the pattern on pages 124-125, cut the apron from striped fabric, extending the lines of the pattern until it reaches the indicated measurements. Allow a 2-cm margin for the hems on the sides, 1 cm along the top of the bib, and 4 cm for the hem at the bottom.

Make a tie (see techniques on page 142) for the neck loop from the shorter strip of polkadot fabric.

Lay the blue polkadot bib facing on top of the bib, right sides together, then insert the ends of the neck loop between the two layers. Following the shape of the apron bib, stitch 1 cm from the edge, securing the ends of the loop in the seam. Trim any excess facing at the sides, then fold the facing to the wrong side of the apron, press and topstitch 1 mm below the top edge of the apron. Turn under 1 cm on the raw edge of the facing and topstitch in place. Pin a piece of rickrack to the front of the apron along this seam and stitch in place.

Press and stitch 1-cm double hems along the remaining curved edge and sides of the apron. Make two ties (see techniques on page 142) from the two remaining strips of polkadot cotton and attach them to either side of the apron at waist level. Press and stitch a 2-cm double hem along the bottom edge.

Press and stitch a 2-cm double hem along one 18-cm edge of the polkadot small pocket. Place this pocket, wrong side down, on the right side of the bottom left corner of the floral fabric. Press under 1 cm on the right-hand edge of the small pocket and topstitch it to the floral pocket. Next, make a 2-cm double hem along the top of the floral pocket and stitch a piece of blue rickrack along the inside so that it shows above the pocket. Turn under 1 cm on the edges of the three other sides, then pin the complete pocket to the front of the apron and topstitch in place. Sew a flat button to the top of the pocket using navy blue thread, to hang a teatowel from, for example.

Floral apron [photo page 47]

1 basic sewing box (see page 6)
1.2 m x 140 cm-wide floral cotton
13 x 2.5 cm strip pink gingham, for the pocket binding, 1 rectangle, 29 x 4.5 cm, for the bib facing, 2 strips, each 70 x 5 cm, for the neck straps, and 2 strips, each 75 x 5 cm for the ties

Following the pattern on pages 126-127, cut the apron from floral cotton, extending the lines of the pattern until it reaches the indicated measurements. Allow a 2-cm margin for the hems on the sides, 1 cm along the top of the bib, and 10 cm for the hem at the bottom. Use tailor's chalk to mark the placement of the darts on the wrong side of the fabric. Baste the darts in position, then stitch.

Cut out the pocket following the pattern, adding a 7-mm margin around the edge. Place the small strip of pink gingham along the top of the pocket, right sides together, and stitch 7 mm inside the edge. Press the seam open, fold the gingham in half towards the inside of the pocket, turn under 7 mm along the raw edge of the gingham and topstitch in place, close to the the edge. Press under 7 mm on the sides and bottom of the pocket then baste and topstitch this pocket to the bib section of the apron.

Make two ties (see techniques on page 142) for the neck straps with the two 70-cm long gingham strips.

Lay the gingham facing section along the top of the apron bib, right sides together, then insert the ends of the neck ties between the two layers. Stitch 1 cm below the top edge, securing the ends of the ties in the seam. Press the seam open. Press and stitch a 1-cm double hem along both curved edges and sides of the apron. Turn the gingham facing to the inside, press under 1 cm along the lower raw edge and stitch in place. Sew over where the ties are attached to reinforce them.

Make the the ties (see techniques on page 142) for the waist in the same way as the neck ties and sew them firmly to each side at waist level.

Press under 2 cm on the bottom edge of the apron, then turn under another 8 cm and stitch the hem in place. Make a 1.5 cm buttonhole on the left side of the apron, as indicated, for inserting one of the waist ties, so the ties can be wrapped and tied at the front.

Brooch [photos pages 47 and 48]

60 x 8 cm strip of fancy print cotton
1 small white fabric flower
small decorations
1 brooch pin

Press the strip of fabric in two, lengthways, wrong sides together. Next, make a few knife pleat folds at one end, overlapping them on the raw edges of the strip so they form the centre of the flower. Hold the middle of the flower firmly in one hand, and continue making a first round of pleated 'petals' around the centre in this way, staggering the base of the pleats a little each time to make gradually larger petals.

Make a second round in the same way, then sew a few stitches by hand around the middle of the flower to hold it all together. Sew a little white fabric flower to the middle, and add decorations of your choice on the petals, then attach the brooch pin to the back.

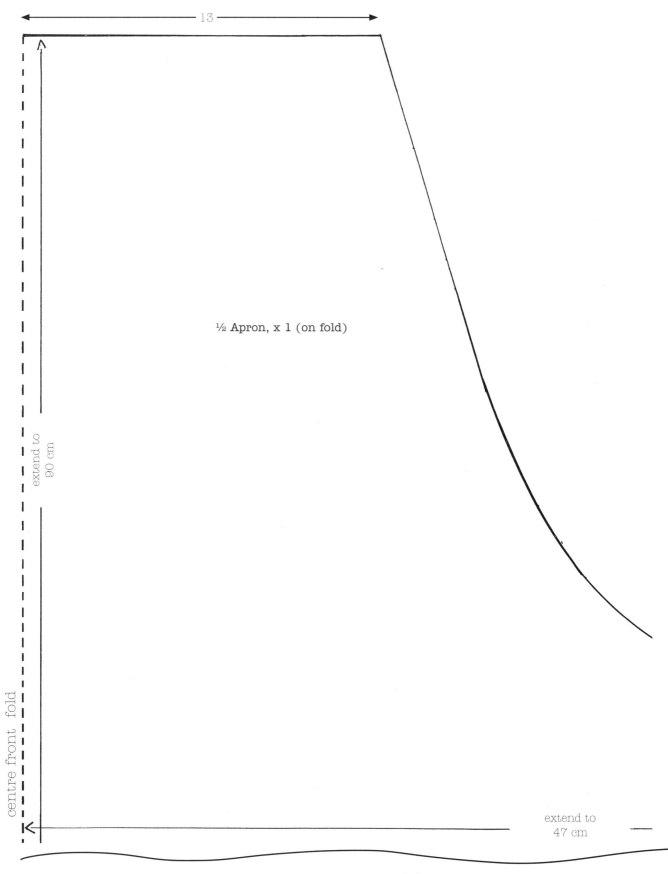

13

½ Apron, x 1 (on fold)

extend to
90 cm

centre front fold

extend to
47 cm

124

instructions
p. 122

Enlarge to 130%

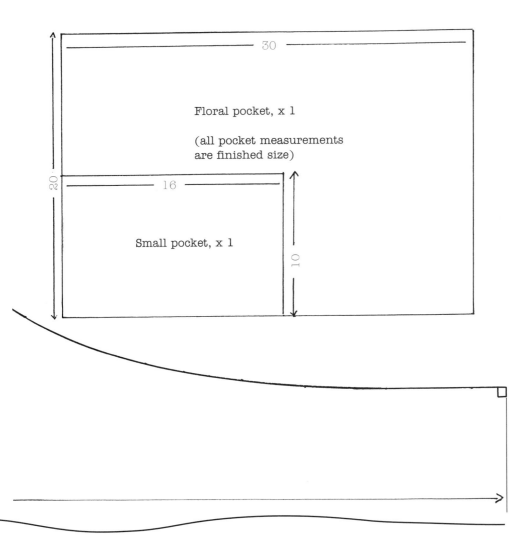

30

Floral pocket, x 1

(all pocket measurements
are finished size)

20

16

Small pocket, x 1

10

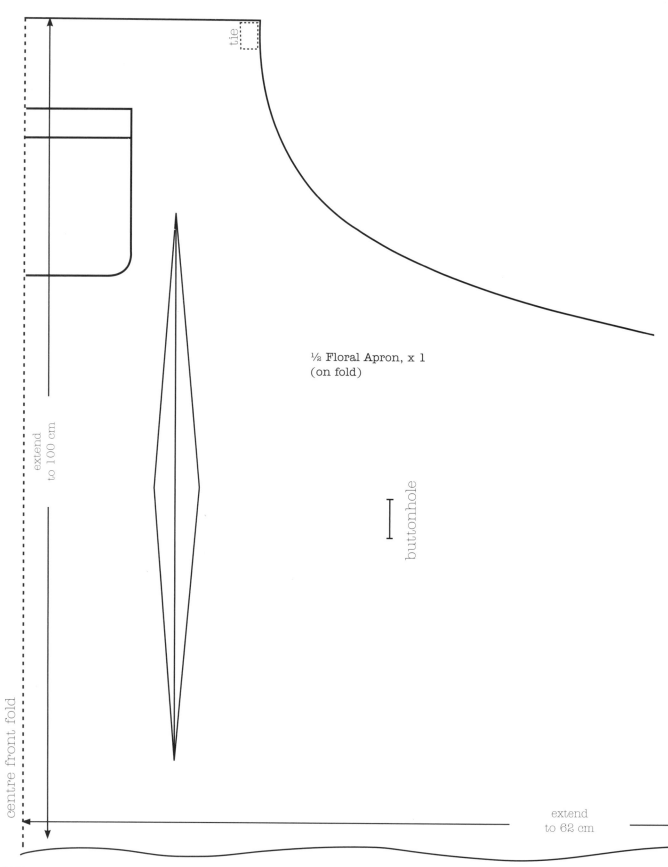

tie

½ Floral Apron, x 1
(on fold)

buttonhole

extend
to 100 cm

centre front fold

extend
to 62 cm

Floral apron

p. 123

Enlarge to 190%

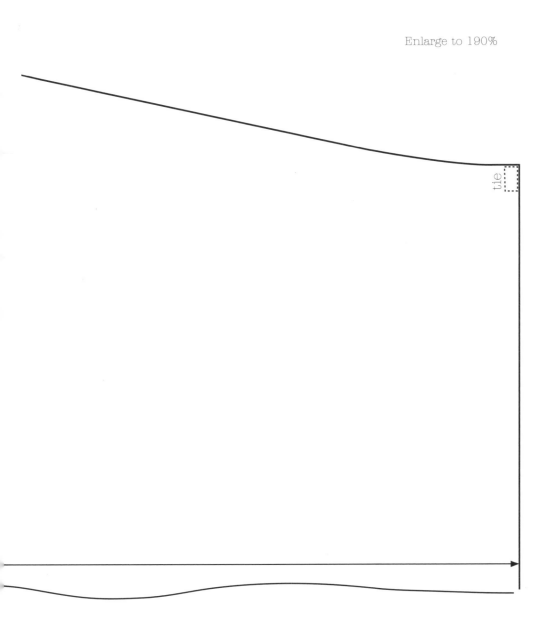

tie

Shoulder bag [photo page 48]

1 basic sewing box (see page 6)
4 rectangles beige-and-white polkadot linen, each 10.5 x 27 cm, for the outside of the bag (1 and 3)
2 rectangles beige floral linen, each 18 x 27 cm, for the outside of the bag (2)
35 cm x 90 cm-wide light fusible wadding
2 rectangles firm red floral cotton, each 35 x 11.5 cm, for the bottom of the bag (5)
2 strips blue-and-white-striped canvas, each 35 x 6 cm, for the top of the bag (4) and 1 rectangle,
    35 x 79 cm, for the lining
2 pieces 15 mm-wide strong beige-and-red-striped reinforced ribbon or webbing

With right sides facing each other and allowing 1-cm seams, sew two rectangles of polkadot linen to either side of a floral linen rectangle along their 27-cm edges (1, 2 and 3 on the diagram below), then press and fuse (see techniques on page 142) a piece of wadding to the wrong side. Next, sew a line of large running stitches by hand, 1 cm inside the seams of the central panel, using two strands of beige stranded cotton.

Fuse some wadding to a piece of red floral fabric (5) and, with right sides together, join it to the bottom edge of the patchwork bag front, stitching 1 cm from the edge. Next, sew a line of large running stitches by hand, 1 cm below the seam, using two strands of beige stranded cotton. Repeat the above process to construct the back of the bag. Pin the back and front pieces together, right sides facing each other. Stitch the sides and the bottom, 1 cm from the edge. To box the lower corners, fold the corner so that the side and bottom seams exactly align. Move a ruler down this folded triangle from the point until the base line measures 5 cm across (2.5 cm on each side of the seam line). Rule a line at this point and stitch across the bag on this line, through both layers. Trim excess fabric below the seam. Repeat for the opposite corner, and turn the bag right side out.

Fuse some wadding to the wrong side of the two strips of striped canvas for the top of the bag. Place the two strips together, right sides facing each other, then stitch the short sides, 1 cm from each edge. With right sides together, side seams matching and raw edges even, stitch the striped section to the top edge of the bag, allowing a 1-cm seam, and press the seam open.

Fold the large rectangle of blue-and-white fabric in half crosswise, right sides together, and stitch the sides, 1 cm from the edges, leaving a 20-cm opening in one side. Box the lower corners in the same way as the outer bag.

Slip the lining bag inside the outer bag, right sides together and seams matching, and pin the upper edges together. Insert a ribbon handle between the two layers at both front and back, positioning the ends 8 cm in from each side. Stitch all around the bag, 1 cm from the edge, catching the ribbon ends in the seam. Turn right side out through the opening. Sew the opening closed by hand or machine and tuck the lining back inside the bag.

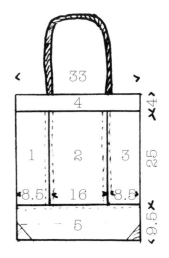

Placement diagram (all measurements are finished size)

Three-pocket tidy [photo page 49]

1 basic sewing box (see page 6)

For the lower pocket

scrap of beige floral linen, to cut a motif and cover buttons
36 x 66 cm beige-and-white polkadot linen, for the outside of the pocket
2 self-cover buttons
36 x 66 cm light fusible wadding
36 x 66 cm beige linen, for the inside of the pocket

For the middle pocket

21 x 16 cm floral linen, for the outer small pocket, plus a small piece to cover the buttons
21 x 16 cm white cotton, for the lining of the outer small pocket
60 cm x 10 mm-wide red gingham cotton ribbon
36 x 66 cm checked linen, for the outside of the pocket
36 x 66 cm beige linen, for the inside of the pocket
36 x 66 cm light fusible wadding
2 self-cover buttons

For the top pocket

36 x 66 cm beige floral linen, for the outside of the pocket
36 x 66 cm light fusible wadding
36 x 66 cm beige linen, for the inside of the pocket
1.6 m x 25 mm-wide beige cotton ribbon
2 self-cover buttons
small piece beige-and-white polkadot linen

Begin with the lower pocket. Cut a motif from the floral fabric in whatever shape you like, then pin it to the centre of the polkadot fabric, 9 cm from the top. Attach it by sewing a border of blanket stitch (see techniques on page 142) all around the edge, using 2 strands of beige stranded cotton. Cover the buttons (see techniques on page 142), using scraps of floral fabric.

Fuse the wadding to the wrong side of the polkadot fabric, then place this rectangle of fabric on the plain beige fabric (see techniques on page 142), right sides together, with the flower motif at the top. Stitch across this top edge, 1 cm from the edge, turn right side out and press.

Place the pocket, motif side down, on your work surface, with the seam at the bottom. Now fold up 29 cm on the bottom edge towards the beige linen, forming a pocket with the flower on the front. Pick up the pocket and fold the polkadot fabric from the back around to the front, folding it back on itself along the lower fold line, so that it sandwiches the smaller pocket between the beige and polkadot layers of fabric. Stitch the sides, 1 cm from the edge, taking the edges of the enclosed pocket into the seams. Turn right side out, then press under 1 cm around the opening top edge and sew closed by hand. Sew a line of large running stitches 2 cm below the pocket opening, using 2 strands of red stranded cotton. Cover two buttons (see techniques on page 142) with floral fabric and sew them to the bottom of the pocket, on each side.

For the middle pocket, place the rectangle of floral fabric on top of the piece of white fabric, right sides together.

Cut the gingham ribbon in half and insert the end of one piece between the two layers in the middle of one long edge. Allowing a 1-cm seam, stitch the pieces together around the edges, catching the end of the ribbon in the seam and leaving a small opening in the other long edge. Turn right side out and press, turning int the raw edges of the opening.

Centre the pocket on top of the checked fabric, 9 cm from the top, and topstitch in place around the sides and bottom, 1 mm from the edge. Sew one end of the other piece of ribbon to the checked fabric, to correspond with the ribbon on the small pocket, so it can be tied closed. Construct the remainder of the pocket as for the lower pocket, using the beige linen and the checked linen. Cover two buttons (see techniques on page 142) with floral fabric.

Place the bottom edge of the middle pocket over the top of the lower pocket, so that it overlaps by 3 cm, and attach the pockets by sewing a button on each side. Sew a few stitches in the centre, to attach the back of the middle pocket to the front of the lower pocket.

Make the top pocket in exactly the same way as the lower pocket but, at the point when you would sew the top closed by hand, cut the ribbon in half, fold each piece in two and insert the folded end into the opening on each side, 1 cm from the edge. Sew a line of fine stitches by hand. Cover two buttons with polkadot fabric, and attach this pocket to the top edge of the middle pocket, as for the other pockets.

Square cushion [photo page 50]

1 basic sewing box (see page 6)

2 rectangles white small floral print cotton, each 7 x 17 cm, for the centre block, and 4 strips, each 22 x 3 cm, for the ties

2 rectangles white-and-red polkadot cotton, each 17 x 7 cm, for the centre block

12 cm square floral fabric, for the centre block

44 cm square red-and-white-striped cotton, for the back, 3 rectangles, each 44 x 13 cm, for the border, and 1 rectangle, 44 x 25 cm, for the border and flap

1 m x 20 mm-wide white lace

44 cm square white cotton, for the front lining

40 cm cushion insert

Make four ties (see techniques on page 142), each 1 cm wide, from the four strips of floral print fabric.

Following the diagram on page 134, sew the small floral print and polkadot rectangles around the floral square, stitching 1 cm from the edges, to make the central block of the cushion front.

Place two of the striped 13 cm-wide rectangles on top of each other, right sides together, laying them out horizontally and making sure to match up the stripes. Place a pin at the bottom edge, 13 cm from the right-hand edge and, using tailor's chalk, trace a diagonal line from this marker out to the top right-hand corner. Stitch along this line, starting 1 cm in from the bottom edge, then trim the fabric back to 1 cm from the seam and press the seam open. Sew the third 13 cm-wide rectangle to one end of the mitred pair in the same way.

Make a 1-cm double hem along one of the long sides of the striped 44 x 25 cm rectangle, then lay this piece of fabric out flat, right side up and hemmed edge at the top. With right sides together, lay one 'arm' of the mitred frame on top, matching up the bottom and the right-hand edges, and making sure the stripes coincide. Measure in 13 cm from the right-hand edge along the bottom and mark with a pin. Using tailor's chalk, trace a diagonal line from this marker to the top right-hand corner of the 13 cm-wide strip. Stitch along this line, starting 1 cm in from the bottom edge, then trim the fabric back to 1 cm from the seam and press the seam open Do the same thing on the left-hand side, placing the pin 13 cm from the left-hand edge: you have now made a mitred frame, with a flap extending on one side.

Pin the centre block to the inside edges of the frame, right sides together, stitch 1 cm from the edge, pivoting at the corners, and press. Topstitch a piece of lace to the right side around the centre block, leaving a 1 cm gap between the lace and the block, so the stripes are visible.

Make a 1-cm double hem on one of the sides of the striped backing square, catching the ends of two ties into the seam, 13 cm from each edge. Lay the cushion front out flat, right side up, with the flap on the left-hand side. Place the cushion back on top, right side down, with the right-hand edges matching and the hemmed edge extending on the left-hand side. Finally, place the lining on top, right side up. Fold the flap back over the lining fabric, making an 11-cm flap. Stitch the sides and the bottom through all layers, 1 cm from the edge, and turn right side out. Topstitch all around the cushion front, 1 cm from the edge, catching the remaining two ties into the stitching, opposite the other ties. Insert a cushion into the cover.

Rectangular cushion [photos pages 51 and 52]

1 basic sewing box (see page 6)
4 strips blue-and-white-striped cotton, each 22 x 3 cm, for the ties
4 squares, each 22 cm, in different red-patterned fabrics
19 cm square of antique white bedsheet or napkin, with a red monogram
12 x 42 cm red-and-white-striped cotton, and 1 rectangle, 13 x 42 cm, for the front
84 cm x 10 mm-wide red rickrack
62 x 42 cm red gingham, for the back, and 20 x 42 cm, for the flap
62 x 42 cm white cotton, for the front lining
pillow insert

Make four ties (see techniques on page 142), each 1 cm wide, from the strips of blue-and-white-striped cotton.

With right sides together and following the diagram on page 134, sew the four squares to each other, stitching 1 cm from the edges. Press under 1 cm all around the edges of the piece of monogrammed fabric, and sew it to the central patchwork panel, using large running stitches and two strands of red stranded cotton. Next, with right sides together and allowoing 1-cm seams, attach the two side panels of striped fabric, catching a piece of red rickrack into each seam and placing the slightly wider panel on the right-hand side.

Lay the cushion front out flat, wrong side up, and place the lining fabric on top, wrong side down, so that the wider striped piece of the front extends beyond the lining. Pin and stitch a 1-cm double hem on the extending striped edge, taking two ties into the seam, 13 cm in from each side, and enclosing the raw edge of the lining in the hem.

For the flap, stitch a 1-cm double hem along one of the long edges of the smaller rectangle of red gingham. Place the flap, right sides together, on the larger gingham backing rectangle, matching raw edges. Insert the remaining two ties between the two layers of fabric, 13 cm from each side, then stitch this seam, 1 cm from the edge, taking the ends of the ties into the seam.

Next, slip the front of the cover and its lining under the flap, lining side up, and stitch around the three other sides.Turn the cover right side out and insert a pillow.

Head-rest [photo pages 51 and 53]

1 basic sewing box (see page 6)
2 rectangles red gingham, each 7 x 32 cm, for the front, 1 rectangle, 14 x 32 cm, for the flap,
   and 4 strips, each 22 x 3 cm, for ties
23 x 32 cm floral cotton, for the front
2 rectangles blue-and-white-striped cotton, each 9 x 32 cm, for the front
64 cm x 10 mm-wide red lace
48 x 32 cm red-and-white-striped cotton, for the back
47 x 32 cm white cotton, for the lining of the front
small pillow insert

Make four ties (see techniques on page 142), each 1 cm wide, with the strips of red gingham.

Following the diagram on page 134 and allowing 1-cm seams, sew the different pieces of fabric for the cushion front together, sewing a piece of lace into the seam on each side of the centre panel.

For the flap, make a 1-cm double hem on one of the long edges of the remaining rectangle of red gingham.

Make a 1-cm double hem on one of the short edges of the striped rectangle for the back of the cushion, catching two ties into the hem, 10 cm in from each side edge.

Baste the lining rectangle to the cushion front around the edges, wrong sides together.

Now lay the cushion front out flat, right side up, and place the two remaining ties on top, raw edges matching and 10 cm in from each side edge. Lay the gingham flap on top, right sides together and raw edges matching, then stitch this seam, 1 cm from the edge, catching the ties in the seam.

Slip the hemmed short side of the striped backing fabric under the flap, with the right side of the backing fabric facing the right side of the front, then stitch the three other sides, 1 cm from the edge, and turn the case right side out. Insert a pillow into the case and tie to secure.

Quilt [photo page 52]

1 basic sewing box (see page 6)
96 squares various cotton prints, each 21 x 21 cm
162 x 242 cm plain cotton, for the backing
170 x 250 cm quilt wadding
8.2 m x 25 mm-wide light-blue bias binding
8.2 m heavy white lace edging

With right sides together and allowing 1-cm seams, sew the squares to each other in rows of eight, to give 12 rows, each 162 cm long. Press the seam allowances for each row in alternate directions. Next, sew the rows together to form the quilt top, which should measure 162 x 242 cm.

Lay the lining fabric out flat, wrong side up, place the wadding on top, then add the patchwork, right side up.

Baste the three layers together carefully. Following the diagram on page 135, quilt the layers (see techniques on page 142), using 2 strands of red stranded cotton, making a four-square grid over the quilt top. Next, trim the wadding to the size of the patchwork.

Stitch the bias binding all around the quilt to finish the edges, then pin the heavy white lace to the right side, all around the edge, and sew it on by hand.

Square cushion

Instructions p. 130

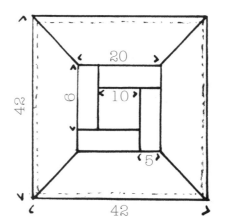

Rectangular cushion

Instructions p. 131

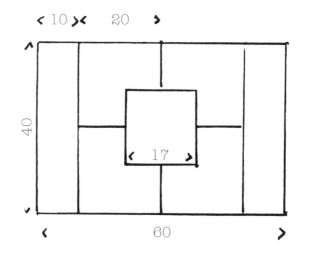

Head-rest

Instructions p. 132

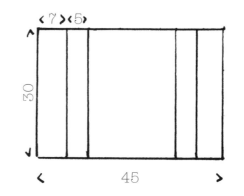

Placement diagrams (all measurements are finished size)

Quilt

Instructions
p. 133

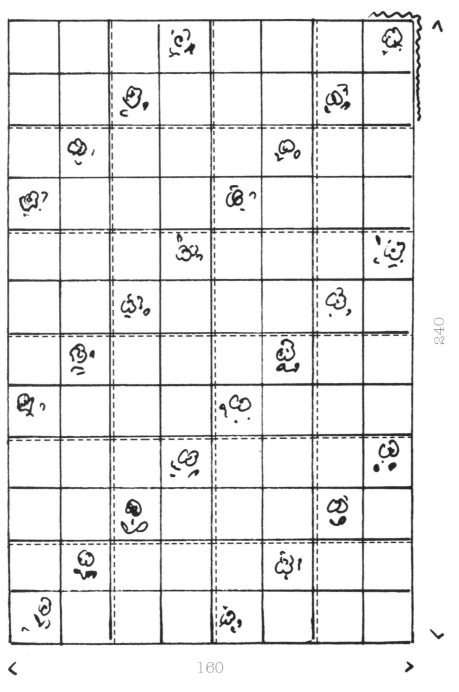

240

‹ 160 ›

Placement diagram (all measurements are finished size)

Laundry bag [photo page 54]

1 basic sewing box (see page 6)
10 pieces of different cotton fabrics for 12 squares, each 13.5 cm x 13.5 cm
48 x 84 cm blue-and-white polkadot cotton, for the back, and 1 rectangle, 48 x 49.5 cm, for the front
50 cm x 10 mm-wide red lace edging
48 x 118 cm white cotton, for the lining, and 2 rectangles, each 13 x 8 cm, for the labels
1 'laundry bag' stamp, 1 '100% cotton' stamp and red indelible ink
1 fabric 'washing instructions' label
1.6 m x 15 mm-wide red cotton ribbon

With right sides facing each other and allowing 1-cm seams, sew the squares together to make three rows of four squares. Press the seam allowances for each row in alternate directions. Sew the rows together, as shown in the diagram below. Stitch the patchwork and the smaller polkadot rectangle together for the front, giving a 48 x 84 cm rectangle. Sew the lace by hand along the seam between the two sections.

Sew the washing instructions label onto one of the patchwork squares. Stamp 'laundry bag' on one rectangle of white cotton and '100 % cotton' on the other, then turn under 1 cm on each edge and sew them to the front of the bag by hand, as pictured, using large running stitches and two strands of red stranded cotton.

Allowing a 1-cm seam and with right sides facing each other, stitch the back and front pieces of the bag together around the sides and the bottom, leaving a 2-cm opening on one side, 18 cm from the top. Fold the fabric for the lining in two, bringing the two shorter edges together, then stitch the sides, leaving an opening in one seam, so you can turn it right side out. With right sides together, pin the top of the bag to the top of the lining, then stitch and turn right side out. Sew the opening closed by hand, push the lining back into the bag and press.

To make the drawstring casing, topstitch the bag and lining together around the opening edge, making two parallel lines of stitching, above and below the side opening. Insert the ribbon into this casing.

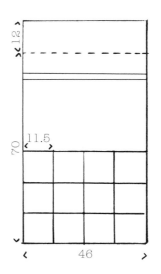

Placement diagram (all measurements are finished size)

Heart sachet [photo page 55]

1 basic sewing box (see page 6)
35 x 15 cm blue-and-white polkadot cotton
8 x 8 cm light fusible wadding
8 x 8 cm floral cotton
a little polyester filling
50 cm x 5 mm-wide red gingham ribbon
1 small white flat 4-hole button

Following the pattern (below) and remembering to add 1 cm seam allowance, cut two large hearts from polkadot cotton. Fuse the wadding to the wrong side of the floral fabric (see techniques on page 142), then cut out a small heart, following the pattern outline without adding seam allowance. Centre the small heart on one of the larger polkadot hearts and sew it in place 3 mm from the edge, using large running stitches with 2 strands of red stranded cotton.

Place the two large hearts together, right sides facing each other, and stitch all around the edge, allowing a 1-cm seam and leaving an opening on one side. Trim the fabric to 3 mm from the seam, then turn the heart right side out, stuff it lightly with polyester filling and sew closed by hand. Quilt around the outside of the heart (see techniques on page 142), about 5 mm from the edge. Tie the gingham ribbon into a pretty bow with long tails. Sew a small white button at the top of the heart using 2 strands of red stranded cotton, catching the ribbon bow in place at the same time.

Enlarge to 130%

Peg bag

Instructions
p. 140

½ Front and Back, x 2 (on fold)

centre fold

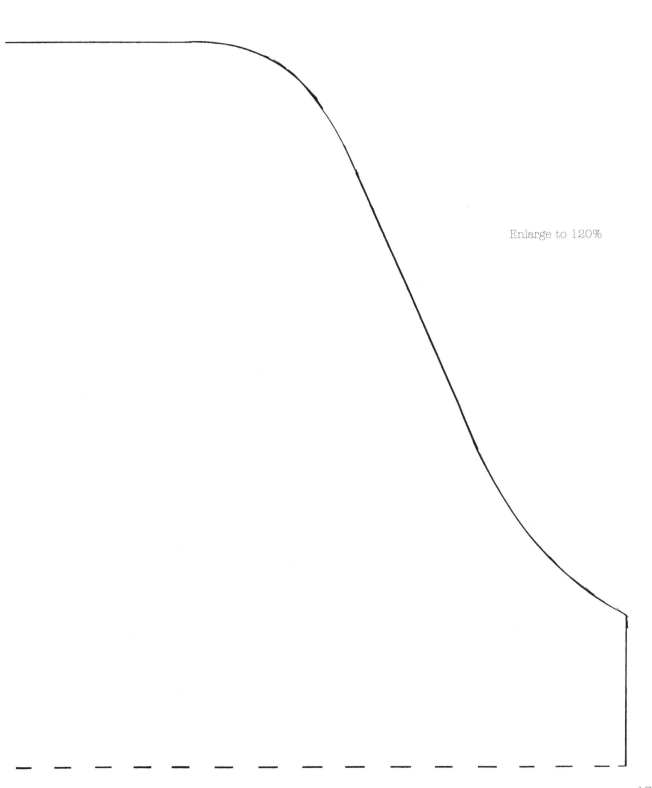

Enlarge to 120%

Peg bag [photo page 56]

1 basic sewing box (see page 6)
1 men's blue shirt, with a chest pocket, for the upper front
1 men's shirt in sky-blue gingham, for the lower front
47 x 45 cm blue-and-white-striped cotton, for the back
47 cm 5 mm-wide red lace edging
10 cm square white cotton
18.5 x 12 cm floral fabric, 18.5 x 12 cm
1 wooden coathanger
4 small white flat 4-hole buttons (cut from the blue shirt)
1 smaller white flat 4-hole button
1 'pegbag' stamp, 1 '100% cotton' stamp and indelible red ink
10.5 cm x 20 mm-wide white twill tape

Carefully unpick the chest pocket from the blue shirt and put it aside. Following the pattern on pages 138-139, cut a piece from the front of the blue shirt, positioning the buttonhole placket along the bottom edge. Make sure you add a 1-cm margin on the sides to allow for the seams and 2 cm at the top for the hem. Topstitch the lace along the bottom of the buttonhole placket.

Cut a 47 x 26 cm rectangle from the front of the gingham shirt, positioning the button band along the top and adding a 1-cm margin along the sides and the bottom to allow for the seams. Using red stranded cotton, sew on the 4 buttons to correspond with the buttonholes. Button the two pieces of fabric together and sew the very small white button to the right of the row of buttons.

Stamp 'pegbag' onto the twill tape and '100% cotton' onto the square of white cotton. Press under 1 cm on each edge of the white square and, using two strands of stranded cotton and large running stitches, sew it by hand onto the chest pocket of the blue shirt, then stitch the pocket onto the gingham rectangle, as shown. Turn under 1 cm on each raw end of the white twill tape and sew it to the top of the pegbag by hand, under the 'neck' opening, using large running stitches and two strands of cotton.

Stitch a 1-cm double hem at the top of the floral fabric rectangle, then press under 1 cm on each of the remaining raw edges and topstitch this piece to the gingham to make a second pocket.

Cut out the striped fabric for the back following the pattern, adding a 1-cm margin to allow for the seams on the sides and the bottom, and a 2-cm margin at the top. Place the back and the front pieces together, right sides facing each other, and stitch the sides and the bottom, 1 cm from the edge. Leave the neck edge open.

Make a 1-cm double hem around the neck opening, then turn right side out thorugh the button opening and slip a coathanger inside.

Drawstring bag [photo page 57]

1 basic sewing box (see page 6)
16 x 18 cm large floral print cotton, for the pocket
16 x 18 cm white cotton, for the pocket lining, and 1 rectangle, 37 x 85 cm, for the bag lining
15 cm x 5 mm-wide red rickrack
2 rectangles blue gingham, each 37 x 27 cm, for the back and front
37 x 35 cm blue-and-white-striped cotton, for the bottom
72 x 20 cm small floral print cotton, for the top, and 1 strip, 120 x 3 cm, for the tie

Place the large floral print rectangle and the 16 x 18 cm white cotton rectangle together, right sides facing each other, and insert the red rickrack between the two layers of fabric along the top, so that the bottom of the rickrack is 1 cm below the edge. Stitch along the top, 1 cm below the edge, catching the rickrack in the seam, then turn right side out and press. Turn under 1 cm along the three remaining sides, and press.

Allowing 1-cm seams, sew a rectangle of gingham on each side of the striped rectangle along the 37-cm edge. Fold the piece in half, bringing the short edges together, finger-press the fold to mark the bottom of the bag, and open out again. Centre the floral pocket on the front of the bag, as shown in the diagram, and topstitch in place along the sides and bottom.

Fold the bag rectangle in half again, right sides together, and stitch the sides, 1 cm from the edge. Turn right side out, turn under 1 cm all around the opening and baste.

Fold the small floral print rectangle in half, bringing the shorter edges together, right sides facing each other, and stitch the short side, 1 cm from the edge, to form a tube, leaving 2.5 cm open at the top of the seam. Press under 1 cm on the raw edges of this opening, then fold the tube in half crosswise, wrong sides together and raw edges matching.Insert the bottom edges of this fabric tube 1 cm inside the opening of the bag and pin in place.

Fold the white lining fabric in half, bringing the two shorter edges together, and stitch the sides, 1 cm from the edge. Insert the lining into the outer bag, fold over 1 cm at the top and topstitch 1 mm from the edge, securing the outside of the bag and the raw edges of the floral fabric in the seam. Next, sew a line of stitching parallel to this seam, on the floral fabric, 7 cm from the top of the bag, to form a casing.

Make a 1 cm-wide tie (see techniques on page 142) from the strip of floral fabric and thread it through the casing.

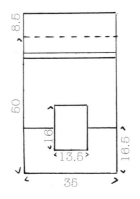

Placement diagram (all measurements are finished size)

techniques

Mitred corners: There are different techniques for creating mitred corners, depending on the effect you want to achieve.

1) To turn a mitred 2-cm double hem on the wrong side of a piece of fabric (such as a placemat or napkin), lay fabric out flat, wrong side up, and press under 1 cm, then another 1 cm, on all edges to mark the hem. Open out the second lot of folds, leaving raw edge folded under. Working on one corner at a time, fold fabric in half diagonally, right sides together, straight edges at top. Rule a diagonal line from the point where the inner pressed fold line meets the diagonal fold, out to the straight pressed edges of the fabric. Stitch along this line, trim excess fabric back to 5 mm from seam and press seam open. Repeat this process on remaining corners, then fold hem back to wrong side on the second pressed fold line and stitch in place by hand or machine. You can also sew some braid or edging along the hem line o nthe right side.

2) To encase the edge of a piece of fabric in a double band with mitred corners on both front and back, you need to cut four strips as follows: cut width should be 2 x desired finished band width, plus 2 cm seam allowance; the length of each strip should be the length of the inner fabric sides (this will be the same for each side on a square, but two different measurements for a rectangle), plus 2 x finished width of band. Press each strip in half lengthways, wrong sides together, with fold at top. Measure in along lower raw edges to a point that is the same measurement as the width of the folded strip. Mark this point with a pin, then rule a line from the pin out to the corner of the folded edge. Cut along this line. Repeat on each end of each strip. Unfold strips and press flat again. Place two strips together, right sides facing each other and raw edges matching (taking care of the order if you are constructing a rectangle). Allowing 1-cm seams, stitch around the pointed ends, pivoting at the point of the triangle and starting and stopping exactly 1 cm from the raw edges. Continue to stitch the ends of the strips together in this way until they are all joined in one continuous 'frame'. With right sides together and raw edges even, pin one raw edge of the band to inner fabric and stitch in place, allowing a 1-cm seam. Turn band right side out and over to wrong side of inner fabric, press under 1 cm on remaining raw edge and stitch in place by hand or machine.

3) To create a single border around a square or rectangle, with mitred corners at the front, you need to cut four strips as follows: cut width should be the desired width, plus 2 cm seam allowance; length should be the desired length, plus 2 x finished width, plus seam allowance. Place two strips on top of each other, right sides together, and fold up the corner until the edges are parallel, then unfold and pin along the fold line. Open out to double-check that your mitre is running in the correct direction, then stitch along the pinned line and trim fabric to 5 mm from the seam and press seam open. Add the other strips in the same way until you have a 'frame', always checking the angle before stitching. Place this frame around the piece of fabric (or on top, depending on the project), and sew on by machine, or by hand, using small invisible stitches. You can also leave 1 cm unstitched at the inner corner of each seam to make it easier to turn under the seam allowance when joining the frame to the inner fabric.

Appliquéing a motif: This is a method of sewing a piece of decorative fabric or a fabric shape onto a piece of backing fabric. There are a couple of ways of appliquéing a motif, depending on the desired effect.

1) Cut your motif or shape from fabric, adding a 5 mm margin all around, then fold under the edge of the fabric 5 mm all around, and pin the motif to the backing fabric. Sew it on by hand, using small, invisible stitches: this is the traditional method of appliqué and results in an appliquéd motif with well-defined edges. If the fabric of the motif is very thin, you can, before sewing it on, fuse some light wadding or interfacing to the back to give it a little more structure.

2) If you want a more 'rustic' motif, with raw edges, first trace your motif onto the paper side of some light double-sided appliqué webbing and cut out roughly, just outside the traced line. (If tracing words or letters, they should be back-to-front.) Fuse the webbing to the wrong side of the fabric, then cut out the motif, cutting accurately along the traced line. Next, remove the backing paper and fuse the motif to the backing fabric. To attach the motif more firmly, you can embroider all around the edge with a stitch that ecompasses the backing fabric and the edge of the motif (such as herringbone stitch, blanket stitch or machine-zigzag), or work a row of running stitch just a few millimetres inside the edge of the motif, using contrasting or matching thread.

Sewing a bias binding: For the projects in this book, we have used the bias binding available in stores which comes with two folded edges. Press open the fold on one side of the bias tape and baste it to the side you want to bind, right sides facing and matching the raw edge of the fabric. Stitch along the crease of the fold, then fold the binding over to the wrong side of the piece, pin in place and sew by hand, using fine stitches.

Sewing in a zipper: Press under the edge on each side where the zipper needs to go and, keeping the zipper closed, pin one edge of the zipper tape beneath the folded edge on one side. Do the same thing for the other side of the zipper, then open the zipper up and stitch along the sides, 1 mm from the edge, using a zipper foot, if sewing by machine. If there is a lining, turn under the edge at the top of the lining, then pin it to the inside of the zipper and sew it in place by hand, using small, fine stitches.

Make a tie: Fold the strip of fabric in half lengthways, right sides together, and stitch along the length and one of the short ends, 1 cm from the edge. Turn right side out with the help of a knitting needle or a small wooden stick, then turn in the fabric on the open end and sew closed by hand with a few invisible stitches. If the ties are too narrow to be turned inside-out, just press under 5 mm on each side and end, fold the fabric in half lengthways, wrong sides together, and topstitch along the edges, 1 mm from the edge.

Make handles: Proceed as for the ties, then press the fabric and, to strengthen them, topstitch along each length on the right side of the fabric, 1 mm from the edge.

Buttonhole stitch: This stitch is worked horizontally, from left to right. If you are embroidering a buttonhole, first embroider the bottom, then turn your work around and embroider the other side. Bring the needle out on the right side of the fabric, to the left of the buttonhole and a few millimetres from the opening. Pass the needle through the slit of the buttonhole, insert the needle into the wrong side of the fabric right beside the exit point of the thread and bring it out on the right side, passing the needle through the loop of thread. Pull delicately on the thread to make sure the stitch lies flat against the fabric, but without pulling too tightly. Continue in the same way, making close, regular stitches.

Blanket stitch: This stitch is worked horizontally, from left to right. Bring the needle out on the right side of the fabric, at the bottom of the motif you want to embroider. Reinsert the needle above and to the right of the exit point of the thread, and bring it out again below, next to the exit point of the thread, passing the needle through the loop of thread. Continue in this way all around the motif. To finish, make a small stitch above the loop of the last blanket stitch.

Stem stitch: This stitch is worked horizontally, from left to right. Bring the needle out on the right side of the fabric, then reinsert to the right and bring out again in the middle of these two points. Keep going in the same way all along the outline to be embroidered, making a continuous line, and always keeping the thread underneath the row of stitches (to the right of the needle).

Quilting: This is a method of sewing several layers together, (such as the fabric for a quilt top, some padding or wadding, and the fabric for the backing of the piece), following an outline so that the stitches create a motif on the fabric. Quilting can be done on the machine or else by hand, with the help of a hoop.

The layers are laid down, nice and flat, and basted together so they don't move, or else held together using safety pins. In this book, the quilts are very easy to make; they mostly follow the outlines of the pieces of patchwork.

Padding and wadding tend to retract when quilted, which is why it is important to always allow a little more than the size of the fabric, and then trim to the size of the work once the quilting is finished.

Covering a button with fabric: First, you need to buy a button-covering kit in a sewing-supplies store, which includes two parts, a rounded metal or plastic part to stretch the fabric over, and another part which fits inside, to hold the fabric in place. If you are comfortable with buying online, you can also find what you want on the internet.

Next, cut a circle from your fabric that needs to be big enough to generously cover the right side of the button and be folded in on the inside. Some very practical kits have a semi-circle outline that you just need to follow for a template. Place the fabric over the rounded part, making sure it is centred and stretched out firmly with no wrinkles, then turn the button over and push the fabric under the inner edge of the button (you can use a small wooden stick or the handle of a brush to do this). Next, fit the second metallic part of the button on by firmly pushing it in.

Using a pattern: If the pattern is actual size, you can just trace it onto tracing paper then cut it out, adding seam allowance if this is indicated. If it needs to be made bigger, enlarge it to the required size (which is indicated on the pattern), then cut it out. For very large pieces, like the aprons, it isn't possible to give the whole pattern in a book.

Here is what you do in that case: transfer the given pattern to tracing paper (or enlarge it to the indicated size) and cut it out, then pin it to your fabric. Next, extend the lines of the pattern on the fabric, using tailor's chalk, until it is the indicated size.

Fusing wadding or interfacing: Place a piece of fusible wadding or interfacing, the same size as the piece of fabric, on the wrong side of the fabric, press, then turn over and iron again on the right side, so the wadding adheres well. For small pieces or particular shapes of fabric, it is simpler to fuse the wadding to a piece of fabric and then cut out the desired shape.

Fusing double-sided appliqué webbing: Double-sided webbing allows you to attach a piece of fabric to a backing fabric, such as for appliqué. Firstly, iron the webbing to the wrong side of the chosen fabric, as for one-sided wadding, then remove the backing paper, position the fabric on the backing fabric and iron so that it adheres. Turn over the whole piece and iron again on the wrong side to improve the hold.

Acknowledgements

Thanks to Lisa, John, Nicolas and all my family, especially my sister Véronique, for all her gifts of vintage fabrics,

To Louise and Monica from Green-Gate, Chantal de Marie and Gustave, for their generosity and their trust,

To Monique, Dominique, Pascale, Frédéric, Vania and Hiriko, for having given life and soul to this book.

First published by Marabout (Hachette Livre) in 2009.
This edition published in 2011 by Murdoch Books Pty Limited

Murdoch Books Australia
Pier 8/9
23 Hickson Road
Millers Point NSW 2000
Phone: +61 (0) 2 8220 2000
Fax: +61 (0)2 8220 2558
www.murdochbooks.com.au

Murdoch Books UK Limited
Erico House, 6th Floor
93–99 Upper Richmond Road
Putney, London SW15 2TG
Phone: +44 (0) 20 8785 5995
Fax: +44 (0) 20 8785 5985
www.murdochbooks.co.uk

Photography: Hiriko Mori
Stylist: Vania Leroy-Thuillier
Design Layout: Frédéric Voisin

Publisher: Diana Hill
Translator: Melissa McMahon
Editor: Georgina Bitcon
Project Editor: Laura Wilson
Production: Joan Beal

National Library of Australia Cataloguing-in-Publication entry
Author: Crasbercu, Corinne.
Title: Made in France: Everything Patchwork/
                 40 classic quilts, bags and accessories
ISBN: 978-1-74196-970-2 (pbk.)
Series   Made in France
Subjects: Patchwork--Handbooks, manuals, etc.
                 Quilting--Handbooks, manuals, etc.
                 Patchwork quilts--Patterns. Bags--Patterns.
                 Dress accessories--Patterns
Dewey Number: 746.46
A catalogue record for this book is available from the British Library.

Printed by 1010 Printing International Limited, China.